I0408965

Revenue optimization for restaurants

Revenue optimization for restaurants
A practical guide for restaurant managers

J. Offergelt

Version 2023

Table of contents

Table of figures

About this book

The restaurant industry is a demanding and dynamic industry with little space for errors. Expenses are high and profit margins are small. The competition is fierce, and it is quite challenging to keep up with the ever-increasing demands of customers.

Managing a restaurant on a day-to-day basis is challenging enough for most owners and managers. Designing menus, forecasting occupancy, marketing the restaurant, keeping up with hygiene protocols, planning of staff and purchasing high quality products at the lowest prices are only a few of the things we need to consider when running a restaurant.

As restaurant managers we should always be looking for ways to increase profits. It does not matter if we are working in a simple take-away restaurant with no seating area or a full-scale three stars classified restaurant, the goal is to make a profit as efficient as possible.

In this book we will discuss the operations finances of the restaurant and more specifically we will talk about how to increase profits. We will do so by having a look at the expenses and revenues and figure out how we can be more efficient.

The approach of this book is practical. We keep things as simple as possible.

Chapter 1
Revenue management

Revenue management has everything to do with taking control of the elements that could have an impact on the revenue streams. By analyzing and taking the right course of action we can save a lot of money, increase sales, and eventually increase profits as well.

Managing a restaurant is not an easy task, but it is not rocket science either. In fact, it is not a science because whatever techniques and strategies we implement, we are not guaranteed of the desired outcomes. We could say that revenue management is more of an art, if done well we might see positive results, but what works on average does not necessarily work for everyone.

When it comes to improving profits, we need to implement a revenue management system. We want to sell the right product, at the right time, to the right customer, for the right price, communicate the right way via the right distribution channel. That sounds like something that is impossible, however if we understand our market and have a solid understanding of the financial side of the restaurant, we can do all those things quite well.

The economic fundamentals of revenue management

To implement a revenue management system, we must understand what the fundamentals are. Not all types of business can implement such a system. There are some boxes to tick off to find out if we can take advantage of revenue management strategies.

The perishability

Perishability means that the product or service we offer can only be sold 1 time and cannot be stored for later use or selling. Therefore, if we do not sell the product today, we cannot sell this product tomorrow (twice). In a restaurant we sell seats. Every seat that is not sold today, cannot be sold an additional time tomorrow to make up for it. The revenue that was lost, is lost forever.

E.g., if we have 100 seats in our restaurant and we sell 80 seats tonight, that means we lose revenue from the unoccupied 20 seats. Tomorrow we once again have 100 seats available, we cannot carry over the unoccupied seats from yesterday.

If we would compare this to a bookshop, then the books that were not sold today can be stored and sold the next day or the day after that. The revenue is not lost forever in this case, it just has not been made yet.

The limited capacity

In line with the previous part, we must understand that a restaurant has a limited capacity (seats) that cannot be easily increased. A restaurant can only accept a certain number of guests during a service and therefore the capacity to service customers is limited. If the square footage has been used right, there is no way that we could just add extra seats. We should already have our tables and seats arranged in the most efficient way.

The distribution of costs

Another element that should be considered is that revenue management needs a business to have low variable costs (ingredients) and the overhead expenses (rent, utilities…) are quite high, up to 80% of all expenses. Every item we sell should cover its own production costs, but also a small part of the overhead expenses. Therefore, the more we sell and the higher the profit margins per sale, the faster we can cover our overhead expenses. What this means is that we should not just accept every customer in our restaurant. We prefer the customers that order a lot of high margin items from the menu. This also means we need to understand our market and therefore the customers.

The market segmentation

This ties in with the previous part which told us we should figure out what clientele we want and what they want from our restaurant. We could have multiple markets or customer groups that all want different things. We need to figure out which markets we can best service. This way we know what customers to accept and which ones to refuse service.

The willingness to pay different prices

To even further make revenue management work for our restaurant we need to have clients that are willing to pay different prices (possibly for the same product). This is why market segments are important. What is means is that some customers are willing to purchase more expensive items, for instance, wine, while others want to buy less expensive wine. The willingness to pay different prices allows us to change prices based on certain conditions, for instance, how far in advance a customer reserves a table or whether the customer wants to have a meal during the afternoon service or the evening service.

E.g., a customer who makes a reservation for the late evening service will pay full prices. However, a customer with a reservation during the afternoon might pay a discounted price for the same items on the menu. This might be because the restaurant has a low occupancy and uses discounted prices to get more customers in during the afternoon service.

As we can see, customers accept the fact that due to certain rules or conditions they might pay a different price for the same thing. This does not work for let us say a supermarket.

E.g., an apple in the supermarket will be same price regardless of when you come to the store. The price will also not be different for people willing to spend more on apples or less on apples nor can we reserve apples beforehand.

The possibility of forecasting

Due to the previous reasons and the uneven distribution of service, we should be able to implement a forecasting system. The uneven distribution means that we do not know how many guests are going to show up at any given time. We do know this because of forecasting.

E.g., during dinner service we have more reservations than during lunch.

E.g., we have more reservations during the summer holidays.

Forecasting allows us to understand and anticipate the demand for our restaurant and allows us to manage the limited capacity and optimize revenue. In other words, we should be able to accept or refuse reservations.

Chapter 2
The pricing rules

In this part will briefly discuss what rules or conditions we can apply to ask a different price for the same service. While we will discuss the more practical way of setting a price on the menu later. Let us have a look at the general reasoning for price setting.

When we decide to set a price, we need to consider many factors, such as the cost prices, salary costs, the competitors, the customers and more. Often, we will set a price in function of the market. Customers usually have a reference of transaction. They know what a specific service in a restaurant should look like. Guests also have a reference of price. Meaning as much as, they know what certain services should cost. The reason for this is that guests usually have been to other restaurants as well and therefore have reference points to what a service should look like and what it should cost. That also means that we need understandable arguments if we want to deviate from these references.

The prices for the services we provide should be fair in the eyes of the customers. If this is not the case it could lead to bad reviews, ill word of mouth and loss of potential future customers and more.

Price discrimination

Implementing price discrimination allows the restaurant manager to ask different prices for the same service to different customers. Price discrimination is accepted by the customers and is implemented in the hospitality industry. This strategy ties in with the fact that different markets are willing to pay different prices. The simplest form of price discrimination is giving discounts to certain market segments. These customers enjoy these benefits purely and only because they belong to a specific market.

E.g., we give students 20% discount.

The tangible price rules

If we want to increase our profits, we should consider changing prices based on tangible rules. Tangible rules are conditions as to why we would ask a different (higher) price for the same service. The importance here is that these rules are tangible, which means as much as that it is clear for everyone why someone pays a different price. It is an explicit rule or condition.

E.g., a group of 20 guests might pay more for the same menu than a group of 40 guests because of the sale volume.

As we can understand from the previous example, most people would understand why the price would be different in this case. We can use tangible price rules to enforce different prices and increase revenue.

The intangible price rules

The intangible price rules are also conditions that allow us to ask a different price for the same service provided. However, these rules are more implicit. Most people know these rules exists but cannot see who has taken advantage of such pricing conditions. Implementing intangible price rules is a necessity for restaurants.

E.g., a customer who makes a reservation 6 months beforehand might get an early reservation discount.

E.g., reservations must be guaranteed with a credit card.

E.g., a customer who makes a reservation once a week might be treated as a V.I.P. and always get the best table near the fireplace.

E.g., menu prices might be discounted during the week.

E.g., walk in guests cannot order à la carte, but must choose a menu.

The price fences

Having all these price rules and conditions in place is extremely important for a restaurant, however we should not just randomly apply these. That is why we should introduce price fences. The price fences are parameters that tell us when we should and should not allow special prices. We could look at it like driving a car. It is a good thing we know how to shift gears, but it is not going to get us anywhere if we do not know when to shift up or down. The same is true for price rules (special prices), we want to open (allow) and close (prohibit) prices.

E.g., we give students 20% discount in our restaurant. However, during the weekend, the restaurant is fully occupied. In other words, we know that customers want to come to our restaurant and pay full price. It would be unfavorable if we had students in our restaurant during this busy high demand period who would ask for the promised discount. In this case we should not ban students, rather we should not allow the student discount during the weekends.

As we can see in the example above it is important to know when to apply special prices. Managing special prices, the wrong way could cost a lot of money. The opposite could also be true, as illustrated in the example below.

E.g., our restaurant is targeting the upper tier of the market, the average price of a menu is €95 per person, and it is considered too expensive for customers in other segments. During the afternoon services we see a significant drop in occupancy. Due to the prestige of our restaurant we refuse to offer any special prices. The fact that we refused to lower the prices during the afternoon, or to offer a different menu caused customers who would have paid a lower price to go to other restaurants in the area instead.

Once again, it has been made clear that having special prices is a good thing, however we need to understand when to apply these prices. The price fence in the first example would ensure that the student discount price would be open from Monday to Friday and closed on Saturday and Sunday. In the second example the price fence would for instance be open Monday to Friday from 12:30pm to 16:30pm and closed during other service hours.

The price level factors

While we do need to take our guests into consideration, we can set prices however we want. If we want to offer prices that are different from the reference price and reference transaction of guest, we can fall back on price level factors.

Price level factors are the arguments we use to justify the prices we ask for our services and products in our restaurant. However, we need to make sure that customers understand the price difference and consider the price to indeed be fair.

E.g., in our restaurant we sell pizza for €99 whereas the competition asks only €19. We ask this high price because we use Italian cheese.

As we can understand from the previous example, no customer will accept this price, nor will they accept the reason as to why we are asking such a high price.

E.g., the prices in our restaurant are 10% higher than the prices of our competitors because we are situated in a monumental building in a unique location.

As we can understand from the example above, customers would understand why prices are higher and will find is very reasonable as well.

Things that might be competitive price level factors include, location, quality of products, experience, image of the restaurant, star classification and price elasticity (how unique and/or replaceable is our service).

Chapter 3
Capacity management

When restaurant managers need to evaluate the success of their restaurant, they mostly do it by referring to the average check as an indicator for success. This is the amount of money a guest spends on average in the restaurant. However, like every other business in the world, a restaurant has potential (maximum) revenue it could achieve.

Optimizing profits can be done by several things (cost control, promotions, price setting, menu engineering, etc.). When we speak of seats in a restaurant, we speak of the capacity. The potential of the restaurant is based on the capacity it holds. The number of seats and the capacity are different things, which we will illustrate in this chapter.

Using the average check to express the success falls flat when it comes to potential. When we say that guests on average spend €50 in the restaurant this sounds great. However, this says nothing about the capacity usage of the establishment.

E.g., today the average check is €120. That is great. However, we only had 1 guest during the 8 hours we were open. The average check is still €120 (total revenue / number of guests). This is terrible in comparison the potential the restaurant has.

To get a better understanding of the revenue, we should instead of average check, refer to the RevPash as an indicator for the success. The RevPash is the revenue per available seat per hour. It combines information from the average check and occupancy of the seats to provide a measurement of the flow of revenue through the restaurant. This way we have a better indication as to how effective the restaurant is using its capacity. To calculate RevPash we can use the following formulas.

Revenue / (number of seats x service hours) = RevPash

Average check x occupancy percentage = RevPash

The average check can be calculated by using the following formulas.

Revenue / number of guests served = average check

Revenue / (number of seats x occupancy rate) = average check

E.g., the restaurant is open for 1 hour. The revenue is €2.400, and we have 80 seats available in the restaurant. This would result in a RevPash of €30 (€2.400 / (80 x 1)). In this case only 70% of the seats were occupied during this hour. This would result in an average check of €42,86 (€2.400 / (80 x 0,7)). That is a lot higher than the RevPash. To find the RevPash again, we can multiply the average check with the occupancy rate (€42,86 x 70%), is €30.

E.g., let us assume the restaurant is open for 2 hours and achieves the same occupancy and revenue. This would result in a RevPash of €15, still, the average check would be €42,86.

In the second example it should be clear that the average check will tell us that all is well, where the RevPash tells us there is a problem. Depending on the type of restaurant, the actual time guests spend in the establishment might vary. In a fine-dining restaurant, guests will be seated longer than in a fast-food restaurant. The longer guests stay in a restaurant (service cycle or duration) the more loss of potential. Since, we cannot sell occupied seats.

The duration control

The service cycle is the total amount of time a guest spends in the restaurant. It is the time it takes for a guest to enter the restaurant, be seated, eat, and drink and eventually leave the restaurant. Reducing the time, a guest stays in the restaurant can increase revenue. Optimizing the service cycle to reduce duration is something that might be interesting.

However, rushing guests through service in a fine-dining restaurant, goes against the whole purpose of fine-dining. While having guests stay longer than one hour in a fast-food restaurant goes against the whole concept of it being fast. When we say, we have 100 seats in the restaurant, and it is open for 2 hours. Theoretically this would mean we can serve 200 (100 x 2) seats (guests) in 2 hours if every guest would spend exactly 1 hour in the restaurant. The maximum capacity would in that case be 200 guests. Most of the time guests will stay for a longer (fine dining) or shorter (fast food) period in a restaurant. This would mean that the average time a guest spends in our restaurant will impact the real potential capacity. Let us assume the service cycle is estimated to be exactly 1 hour. If a guest stays longer than 1 hour, it lowers the maximum capacity. If a guest stays shorter than 1 hour, it will raise the maximum capacity. Since, theoretically there would be less seats and more seats available.

The time a guest spends in a restaurant is called the service cycle time. To find out what it is, we must measure how long guests stay on average.

To calculate the actual maximum capacity, we use the following formula.

(Number of seats x service hours) / service cycle time = maximum capacity

E.g., a restaurant has 80 seats and is open from 6pm until 11pm. On average a guest would spend 54 minutes or 0,9 hours (54 / 60) in the restaurant. The maximum capacity of this restaurant would be 444 seats ((80 x 5) / 0,9). Not 400 seats (80 x 5).

Let us have a look at another example to make it clear why this service cycle is important.

E.g., a restaurant has 100 seats and a revenue of €10.000. The cycle time is 60 minutes. The restaurant is open for 5 hours a day. Let us say the restaurant works at 100% occupancy all the time (high in demand). In total 500 guests were served. The average check would be equal to the RevPash (this is the ideal world). Average check is €20 (€10.000 / 500 guests).

The RevPash is also €20 (€10.000 / (100 x 5)). We found a way to make the service cycle more efficient by 2 minutes. This would mean a guest would stay 58 minutes instead of 60 minutes. This would let us potentially serve 17 more guests.

60 minutes x 5 hours = 300 minutes of service hours.

(300 / 58) x 100 = 517,24 ≈ 517 total guests served.

517 – 500 = 17 extra guests.

As we can understand, making the service cycle more efficient is an interesting idea and it should be done if we can. However, it is quite difficult to manage since we are in the service industry and are working with people. We are selling dinner, lunch, meals, beverages, seats, etc. The duration of a customer in our restaurant is still uncertain. There will always be people that spend more time or less time in the restaurant regardless of how efficient the service cycle is.

To potentially fix this problem we could implement timeslots to ensure that a customer spends only a predetermined amount of time in our restaurant. This allows us to take control of the uncertainty of duration and allows us to more efficiently schedule reservations and increase potential profits because we know exactly when a customer is checking in and checking out of the restaurant.

While this might not be as important in a fine-dining restaurant, where we do not necessarily want a high seat turnover, we can understand the importance of this cycle for fast food restaurants.

The table and seating mix

Sometimes the actual tables and seats are the problem in a restaurant. Not having the right mix or combinations will cost money. Have you ever noticed people walking in, looking, and decide 'their' table is not there and walk out. Or you have had groups walk in and you needed to rearrange everything to make sure that party will stay. If things like this happen often, you might have the wrong table and seating mix. That is exactly why it is important to understand how it works.

The table and seating mix is nothing more than figuring out the party sizes of guests that come to the restaurant. The next thing we should do is arrange and adjust the restaurant' tables and seats accordingly. If we only have parties of 2 persons walk in, we have no need for 4 persons and 6 persons tables.

To get a better understanding of the parties coming to the restaurant, we must count and take notes. We can check the historical data of the reservations and have a look at the competitors. The concept of this mix is simple, and it can be done in a few simple steps. We will explain this with an example.

E.g., a restaurant has 100 seats. We have calculated the following for the different parties. Party of 1 or 2, 50% of the time. Party of 3 or 4, 30% of the time. Party of 5 or 6, 20% of the time. Let us say during this timed period, the restaurant served 100 parties.

Numbers of parties and their sizes

50% of 100 parties = 50 parties of 1 or 2 persons. 30% of 100 parties = 30 parties of 3 or 4 persons. 20% of 100 parties = 20 parties of 5 or 6 persons.

Deciding on the table sizes

Parties of 1 can sit at a 2 person's table. Parties of 3 can sit at a 4 persons table, etc. So, we always count 2 seats per table unless there is a reason not to do so.

50 parties at a 2 persons table = 50 x 2 = 100 seats. 30 parties at a 4 persons table = 30 x 4 = 120 seats. 20 parties at a 6 persons table = 20 x 6 = 120 seats.

So, we would need a total of 340 seats (100 + 120 + 120). We only have 100 seats; we need to convert this number to 100 seats for our restaurant.

The conversion of seats to percentages

2 persons table = 100 / 340 = 29,41% ≈ 30%. 4 persons table = 120 / 340 = 35,29% ≈ 35%. 6 persons table = 120 / 340 = 35,29% ≈ 35%.

The conversion of the number of seats per table size

Now we can translate the previous steps to our restaurant.

2 persons table = 30% x 100 = 30 seats.
4 persons table = 35% x 100 = 35 seats.
6 persons table = 35% x 100 = 35 seats.

The conversion to tables

30 seats / 2 persons = 15 tables (15 x 2 = 30)
35 seats / 4 persons = 8,75 tables ≈ 10 (10 x 4 = 40)
35 seats / 6 persons = 5,83 tables ≈ 5 (5 x 6 = 30)

These numbers do not always line up nicely because we cannot place 5,83 parts of a table and so on. Therefore, we need to round up and round down accordingly to make sure the tables correspond with the available seats.

In this case we need to have a total of 100 seats. We choose to round up the 4 person's table. We could have decided to round up differently (17 x 2 and 9 x4 instead, would have given us also a total of 100 seats).

This would be the most optimal mix for tables and seats for this restaurant. This ensures the highest chance that at any given time we must have the optimal mix for our guests available, and do not have to turn customers away.

Chapter 4
Forecasting

Taking control of the restaurant also means that we need to look into the future to anticipate what might happen and adjust our operations accordingly. To do this we need to make forecasts. A forecast allows us to understand what might happen at any given moment in time. If we know what is going to happen, we can determine how much revenue we receive, how many expenses there are going to be and what to do with the profits. We can also schedule staff, open and close special prices, decide what ingredients to order and set a budget that we can later compare with the actual results. Forecasting is of vital importance to a restaurant; without a forecast it will be extremely difficult to manage a restaurant well.

We will not go into detail on how to set up a forecast however we will have a look at a simple example.

In the figure below we can see the number of guests served in the previous 4 weeks, for the weekdays. We can also find the average number of guests per week and per day of the week. Lastly, we see what the average spending per guest was per day of the week.

	Week 1	Week 2	Week 3	Week 4	Total	Average	Average check
Monday	375	390	345	385	1495	374 €	42,00
Tuesday	300	310	305	325	1240	310 €	35,00
Wednesday	310	315	325	295	1245	311 €	37,00
Thursday	405	415	390	405	1615	404 €	44,00
Friday	455	475	445	465	1840	460 €	51,00
Total	1845	1905	1810	1875			
Average	369	381	362	375			

Figure 1: the guests forecast and average spending.

If we were to make a simple forecast for week 5, we could simply say that for the Monday in week 5 we would expect 374 guests (because this is the average number of guests over 4 for weeks of data). Those 374 guests should generate a revenue of €15.708 (374 x €42). We could also assume that for week 6, 7 and 8 the average number of guests would be 374 as well.

We can also see and expect a drop in sales on Tuesdays and Wednesdays, therefore we might want to introduce special menu prices to bring more customers into the restaurant. The point is that the forecast is a crucial tool to manage the restaurant. There is no need for advanced software and complex calculations, we can simply use the historical data as a guideline and adjust it day by day, week by week and incorporate additional information.

E.g., we would expect 374 guests on Monday in week 5. We also know that the weather in the previous weeks was bad, and in week 5 it is expected to be much better. Also, a new museum is opening on that day. We can expect more customers. How much we do not know. We can look at other historical data of our restaurant. We use our best day (Friday) as a guideline and adjust the number of guests on Monday from 374 to 450.

With this forecast ready, we are much better prepared for the upcoming week.

The reservations curve

Keeping track of data is important if we want to make forecasts and compare current results to previous results. We can compare this month to previous month or the same month last year and so on. The sky is the limit if we have the data available. Some important data to keep track of would include, average check, number of guests, cancelations, no-shows, and the reservation curve.

The reservations curve allows us to understand how the reservations are evolving compared to a previous period. By tracking the reservations curve we can easily spot if we are on target or not. If we are not, we can take action to bring the curve in line with our estimations or previous results.

Days before arrival	Bookings	Seats reserved	Occupancy
Monday 7	19	37	25%
Tuesday 6	29	66	44%
Wednesday 5	23	89	59%
Thursday 4	16	105	70%
Friday 3	15	120	80%
Saturday 2	17	137	91%
Sunday 1	9	146	97%
Monday 0	0	146	97%

Figure 2: the reservations curves occupancy overview.

In the figure above we can see the reservations from the past week. Monday 0 is today. Today we received 0 bookings for today, we received 9 reservations on Sunday 1 (yesterday), for today (Monday 0).

To clarify, this figure shows only the reservations made on each day for Monday 0. If we want to see the reservations for upcoming Tuesday (tomorrow) we would get a similar overview as well. To be precise, we would have 365 of these overviews (for every day of the year).

Let us assume that today is Monday 7 (7 days before Monday 0). Now we are one week in advance to figure out if we are on track. Today we have received 19 reservations for Monday 0 next week, bringing the total occupancy up to 25%.

Let us assume that Monday 7 has passed and today we are Tuesday 6 (6 days before Monday 0). Today we have received 29 reservations for Monday 0. If we add up these reservations with the reservations we already have, then that would bring the total number of reservations (seats) to 66 (37 +29).

We do the same for Wednesday 5 and that would bring the total number of reservations for Monday 0 to 89 (66 + 23). We keep repeating this until we reach Monday 0, where we can see the result.

The occupancies change per day because we receive reservations and have cancellations for a specific day. But also depending on the day we are right now and at which day we are looking we will see different numbers. Usually over time, the closer we are to the day we are looking at the higher the occupancy.

	Thursday 4	Friday 3	Saturday 2	Sunday 1	Monday 0
Wednesday 5	91%	85%	71%	65%	59%

	Friday 3	Saturday 2	Sunday 1	Monday 0
Thursday 4	92%	88%	71%	70%

	Saturday 2	Sunday 1	Monday 0
Friday 3	95%	92%	80%

	Sunday 1	Monday 0
Saturday 2	94%	91%

	Monday 0
Sunday 1	97%

	Today
Monday 0	97%

Figure 3: the reservations overview per day of the week.

In the figure above we can see how the occupancy evolves day per day. If on Wednesday 5 we look at the upcoming 5 days, we could see something like this. On Thursday 4 we have 91% occupancy and 59% for Monday 0. If we arrive on Thursday 4, we see that the occupancies for all the days went up because we have received reservations from customers for different days of the week.

If we go back to the example for Monday 0, we can see that the occupancy changes every day that we look at this overview.

The problem here is that we only know if we achieved our goal on Monday 0 on that day itself. We have no understanding of whether the reservations were going in the preferred direction or not. We can see the occupancy increasing day by day, but we do not know if that is good or not. The same goes for other days of the week. We do not know if having 59% occupancy for Monday 0 by Wednesday 5 is good or not.

Lucky for us the occupancy was 97% which is not that bad of course. But what if it was 40%? Then we are too late to act. While a week beforehand we could have done something, for instance with the prices to attract more customers for Monday 0.

Obviously, we would need to start looking at this reservation curve earlier but also, we need to compare the results this week, this month, or this year with previous periods to really understand if we are doing better or worse.

If we look at the reservations for the same period last year, we get a better understanding of what is going on with our bookings.

Days before arrival	Bookings	Seats reserved	Occupancy
Monday 7	21	49	33%
Tuesday 6	29	78	52%
Wednesday 5	22	100	67%
Thursday 4	23	123	82%
Friday 3	16	139	93%
Saturday 2	11	150	100%
Sunday 1	0	150	100%
Monday 0	0	150	100%

Figure 4: the reservations overview for Monday 0.

In the figure above we see the booking curve for the same week last year. In the previous year we had more reservations on the books day per day, but also the actual day (Monday 0) we were fully booked at 100%. If we had this information, we might have been able to see this difference and intervene.

In the figure below we can see the difference in reservations on the books (seats reserved) on a day-to-day basis. By Tuesday 6 and/or Wednesday 5, it should have been clear that reservations were falling behind, compared to the previous year.

	This year	Previous year	Variance
Monday 7	37	49	-12
Tuesday 6	66	78	-12
Wednesday 5	89	100	-11
Thursday 4	105	123	-18
Friday 3	120	139	-19
Saturday 2	137	150	-13
Sunday 1	146	150	-4
Monday 0	146	150	-4

Figure 5: the reservations variance.

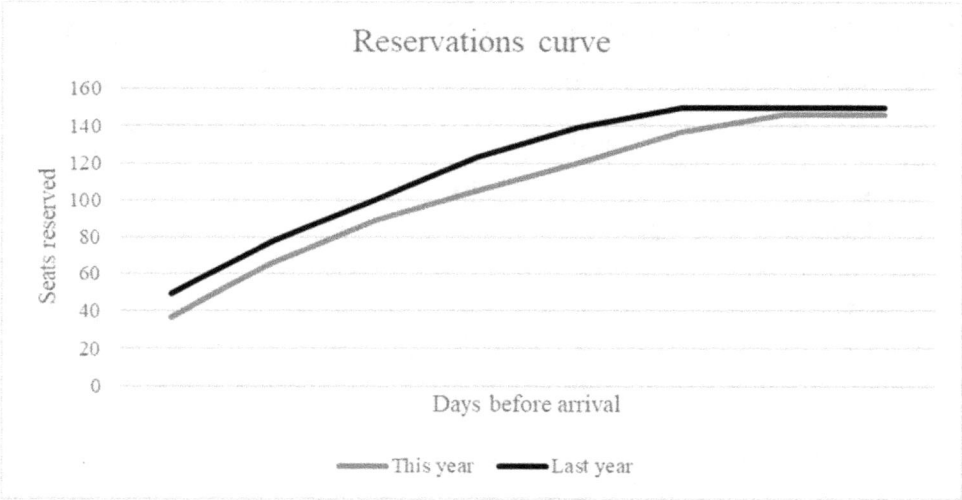

Figure 6: the graph of the reservations curve.

In the figure above we have the visual representation of the reservations per year for Monday 0. It is easy to see the gap between last year and this year. As we can understand it is important to keep track of and compare the reservations curve to intervene swiftly with the right sales and marketing strategies to maximize profits.

Hot hours and cold hours management

Managing busy moments also known as hot hours and managing slow periods also known as cold hours the right way can help improve profits. Taking control of hot- and cold hours is not that difficult in terms of the strategies that we should apply and luckily, it is quite easy to determine what moments in a restaurant could be considered hot and cold.

Hot hours are periods that have a higher occupancy rate, higher average check and higher RevPash compared to other periods. For cold hours this is the exact opposite. To understand if a certain period is hot or cold, we need to determine the occupancy rate, average check and RevPash per period. Because hot- and cold hours are usually short-lived moments we want to reduce the timeframes significantly. A period in this instance is 1 hour or 60 minutes.

E.g., our restaurant has 100 seats, is open Monday to Friday from 12PM until 10PM (10 hours). In total the restaurant has 50 service hours per week and 5.000 seats available of which 3.000 were occupied.

	12:00 PM	1:00 PM	2:00 PM	3:00 PM	4:00 PM	5:00 PM	6:00 PM	7:00 PM	8:00 PM	9:00 PM	10:00 PM
Monday	€ 2,15	€ 2,31	€ 2,63	€ 5,83	€ 1,93	€ 3,55	€ 3,66	€ 4,11	€ 3,91	€ 3,42	
Tuesday	€ 3,19	€ 3,11	€ 2,75	€ 2,89	€ 3,66	€ 5,11	€ 4,98	€ 4,87	€ 5,12	€ 3,12	
Wednesday	€ 4,75	€ 4,20	€ 4,11	€ 3,78	€ 4,99	€ 4,63	€ 2,30	€ 2,71	€ 3,10	€ 3,93	
Thursday	€ 4,30	€ 3,89	€ 3,51	€ 2,64	€ 4,89	€ 4,78	€ 1,36	€ 1,58	€ 1,99	€ 4,70	
Friday	€ 2,90	€ 2,99	€ 2,78	€ 3,88	€ 3,45	€ 3,67	€ 3,89	€ 4,12	€ 4,15	€ 5,80	
	€ 17,29	€ 16,50	€ 15,78	€ 19,02	€ 18,92	€ 21,74	€ 16,19	€ 17,39	€ 18,27	€ 20,97	
										€ 182,07	
									RevPASH	€ 3,64	
				100	Seats				Total revenue	€ 18.207,00	
				50	Hours				Average check	€ 6,07	
				5000	Total seats				Occupancy	60%	
				3000	Guests				Hot	€ 4,55	+25%
									Cold	€ 2,73	-25%

Figure 7: the hot- and cold hours weekly overview.

The total revenue for this week is €18.207.

The RevPash is €3,64 (€18.207 / 5.000).

The average check is €6,07 (€18.207 / 3.000).

The occupancy rate is 60% ((3.000 / 5.000) x 100).

To decide which hours are hot and which ones are considered cold we use the RevPash. Therefore, we could consider all hours with a RevPash of more than €3,64 hot and hours with a RevPash of less than €3,64 cold. This reasoning is not per definition wrong, but what about borderline revenues? Is a RevPash of €3,63 cold? And can we consider a revenue of €3,65 hot?

To exclude borderline revenues, we can choose a value that is noticeably higher or lower. In this case we decided that 25% more and 25% less than the RevPash would be considered a hot hour or cold hour.

Hours with a RevPash of €4,55 (€3,64 x 1,25) are hot hours. Hours with a RevPash of €2,73 (€3,64 x 0,75) are cold hours.

Once we have decided which hours are considered hot and cold, we can highlight these on the overview and make some decisions to increase our profits.

Hot hours management

- *Optimize seating and table mix.*

- *Offer a smaller menu.*

- *Implement menu engineering and offer items with a high profit margin.*

- *Increase prices during these hours.*

- *Price fences should be up (no discounts are allowed).*

- *Don't accept reservations during this period (enough walk ins).*

- *If reservations are accepted then guests must pay in advance.*

- *Restrictions on hold time (no longer than 15min after expected arrival time).*

- *No suggestions or only limited suggestions (it takes too much time).*

- *Focus on increasing seat turnover not on increasing the average check.*

Cold hours management

- *Optimize seating and table mix.*

- *Offer a larger menu.*

- *Price fences should be open to allow for price discrimination.*

- *Discounts for all customers.*

- *Offer promotion menus.*

- *Introduce happy hour.*

- *Accept reservations without payment in advance.*

- *Restrictions are less strict.*

The displacement costs

Because we are limited in our capacity, we cannot always offer every guest a seat in our restaurant, and since we cannot increase the capacity, we must make choices. We must decide who gets to eat in our restaurant and who we turn away. When it comes to guests walking into the restaurant, we usually take on the first come first served approach. We will make exceptions for special guests and guests with reservations of course. When it comes to taking reservations or choosing whether to accept a group it might be more difficult to make such a decision.

To help us make the right decision we need to calculate the displacement costs, what we can only do if we have a good forecast and tracking of the reservations curve. We need to know how many cancellations we expect, how many walk ins there will be, what type of guests we expect (big spenders or not), etc. To determine which customers to accept we are going to have a look at the revenue specifically and decide based on who brings in more money. However, we might have to consider other elements as well, such as, the preparation time, table setup, service cycle, preferred guests, previous visits, special requests and more.

Groups versus individuals

If we choose to accept a group which usually pays less per person than a walk-in guest, we need to make sure that we recover the losses of not being able to serve said walk in. We need to find out if we generate more money from this group or not. Because we have an idea of what walk in spends on average, and based on the forecast we know what we could expect on a certain day. If the group does not at least make the same amount of money, there is no reason to accept the reservation (because we would make a loss).

Seats available	150	Request	
Average check	€ 55,00	Seats	30
Cost of food & beverage	€ 16,50		
Contribution margin	€ 38,50		

Day	Forecast	Group seats	Displacement	
Monday	135	30	15	
	Total	30	15	Displaced seats
		€	577,50	Displaced contribution margin
		€	577,50	Difference in contribution needed
		€	35,75	Minimum average check

Figure 8: the calculation of the displacement cost.

In the figure above we can see that we received a request from a group of 30 people. Guests in our restaurant spend on average €55 (average check) and provide us with a contribution margin or profit margin of €38,50 (average check €55 – the cost of production €16,50).

The restaurant has a seating capacity of 150 and the forecast tells us that 135 of those seats will be occupied on the requested day. We assume there will be no additional individual guests arriving on that day.

Theoretically we could only accept 15 guests of said group (150 – 135). That would leave us with 15 group guests that would not have a seat in our restaurant. This means we need to refuse or cancel 15 reservations of individual guests in favor of the 15 group guests who do not have a seat right now. This is what is called a displacement, in this case a displacement of 15.

Since we are a restaurant, we assume there are no other services or products we sell to generate additional revenue in favor of the group, such as meeting space revenue or room revenue (hotels).

We would have to refuse 15 individual guest @ €38,50 contribution margin each, for a total of €577,50 (€38,50 x 15). This means that the group needs to provide at least €577,50 in contribution margin to bring in the exact amount of money as the 15 displaced individual guests would have. If that is the case it would not matter if we accepted the group or the individuals, purely based on finances.

The price we should at least ask per person from this group is €35,75 ((€577,50 / 30) + €16,50).

The group would pay €1.072,50 (€35,75 x 30) + VAT.

We assume that the menu of this group also costs €16,50 per person. Therefore, the cost of ingredients would be €495 (€16,50 x 30). And the total contribution margin would be €577,50 (€1.072,50 - €495).

If the group would order a menu that is cheaper to produce, the profit margin would be higher, and the group would be preferred over the individual guests. We could also ask a higher menu price per person of course.

Groups versus groups

The same questions arise when deciding which group to accept in the restaurant. Here, we also must take all the elements into consideration to make an informed decision. In the case of groups, we should also calculate displacement costs, or simply compare the groups. We can use the same method as previously discussed if we have a group that wants to eat à la carte versus a group that wants a menu. Then we would treat the à la carte group as if they were individual guests.

When dealing with groups we usually offer several menus, or guests will inform us on what the menu should look like and what they would like to spend.

	Group A	Group B
Seats	55	70
Menu price	€ 50,00	€ 35,00
Revenue	€ 2.750,00	€ 2.450,00
Cost of food and beverage 30%	€ 825,00	€ 735,00
Total contribution margin	€ 1.925,00	€ 1.715,00

Figure 9: the displacement costs between groups.

In the figure above we have 2 groups. Group A is 55 guests and want to spend €50 on a menu (let us say menu 1) with an ingredient cost of 30%. Group B is 70 guests, but they will only spend €35 on a menu, also with an ingredient cost of 30%. Based on the numbers we can easily figure out which group generates more profit.

The revenue for group A is €2.750 (€50 x 55) and €2.450 (€35 x 70) for group B. The food cost is 30% for both groups. That means it will cost us €825 (€2.750 x 30%) to produce menu one and €735 (€2.450 x 30%) to produce menu 2. If we subtract the cost of food and beverage from the revenue, we find the contribution margins or profits per group.

Group A will generate a profit of €1.925 (€2.750 – €825) and group B will generate a revenue of €1.715 (€2.450 – €735). In this case we should accept the reservation from group A.

Let us assume that the menus each have a different production cost (food cost and beverage cost). What would happen if menu 1 would be more expensive to produce (40% food- and beverage cost) and menu 2 would stay the same.

		Group A	Group B
Seats		55	70
Menu price		€ 50,00	€ 35,00
Revenue		€ 2.750,00	€ 2.450,00
Cost of food and beverage	40 and 30%	€ 1.100,00	€ 735,00
Total contribution margin		€ 1.650,00	€ 1.715,00

Figure 10: the displacement cost for groups with different food costs.

As we can see, if the cost of production would be different, we would get a different outcome, and we would accept group B instead of group A.

Chapter 5
Cost control

Expenses or costs are all the payments that need to be made to keep the restaurant operational. The most common expense we think about when running a restaurant are the purchases of ingredients. However, there is more as we know. Before we continue, let us clarify what expenses mean.

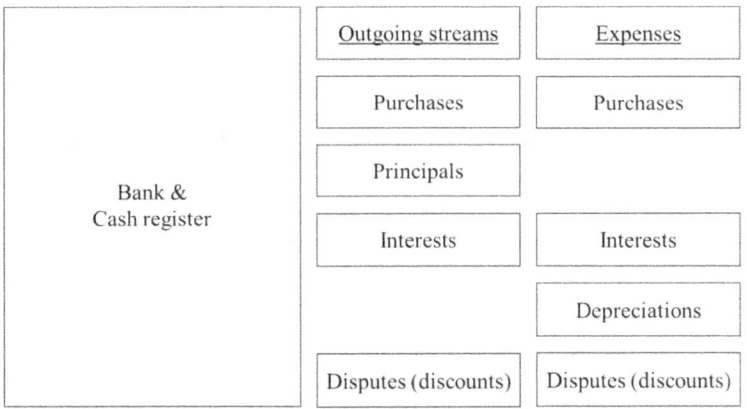

Figure 11: the overview of outgoing money streams and expenses.

To define what we are talking about let us make a distinction between outgoing money streams and expenses. Because not all outgoing money streams are an expense and not all expenses have an outgoing money stream.

Outgoing money streams (outgoing streams) mean all money that leaves the restaurant either via the bank account or the cash register. It does not really matter why this money leaves the business or how and to whom, the fact of the matter is, money has left our restaurant. When there is a money stream, be it going out or coming in, it will have an impact on the cashflow. Money that has transferred from the restaurant will have a negative impact on the cashflow, since this money cannot be used for other payments (we do not have it anymore). The opposite it also true.

- *E.g., we pay an invoice from our supplier.*

- *E.g., we pay back an unsatisfied customer.*

- *E.g., we pay an installment from a business loan or credit card.*

- *E.g., we pay an interest as part of the monthly installments from a loan.*

In all the previous examples money does leave the restaurant. However, paying back installments of a loan is not an expense, the expense part or cost of a loan is the interest. And lastly there are the depreciations. A depreciation is an expense, but it is not an outgoing stream of money since no money will be transferred.

We will discuss the direct costs such as purchasing costs of food and beverage, direct staffing costs in more detail.

The cost of food and beverage

If we have a restaurant or a similar business in the food service industry, we need to learn about food cost and beverage cost. Learning about how it works and knowing how to apply it will be one of the more common and useful ways of maintaining control over important direct costs. The food cost and beverage cost are two key performance indicators that tell us instantly how well we are doing in terms of controlling the direct expenses related to the production of meals (food) and drinks (beverage). These indicators however do not tell the whole story about how well the restaurant is doing, but it will give us an indication.

The food cost and beverage costs are key tools that indicate the relationship between the costs of the food and the costs of beverage usage in comparison to the turnover created in the restaurant.

The same principle as in any other business applies here. Costs should be reduced to the absolute minimum, always, with no or minimum impact to the experiences of our guests. Reducing costs in principle is straightforward and not that difficult. The impact of reducing the costs might have a substantial impact on the experiences of our guests. To a certain extent it might have a significant impact on staff as well.

E.g., to reduce energy costs, we turn off the heating during the winter.

As we can imagine in the previous example, we would save a lot of money from this cost reduction. But guests and employees will stay away from our restaurant, thus, costing us more than if we would leave the heating on an generate revenue. This, of course is a silly example, but it drives home the point that we should make smart decisions when it comes to taking control of our expenses. If we would use an example more related to the subject of food and beverages, then we could reduce costs by using ingredients of lesser quality.

When it comes to purchasing ingredients it all comes down to buying the highest quality at the lowest price. Unfortunately, to get the highest quality we will have to pay top dollar. Spending more on high quality products should not be a problem at all, we can of course translate this to the sales price of an item on the menu.

Implementing an efficient cost management system will give us an advantage over competitors who do not use such a system. If not this, then it will at least assist us in increasing revenues for our restaurant. Implementing a cost control system sounds like it is difficult to do. Fortunately, it is quite simple to start, it just takes time to set it up. The first thing to implement is, cost control. Cost controlling, but all the other techniques we will discuss can be applied to different outlets within an establishment if needed, and it can be made as complex as we want. We should try to make it as simple as possible and make sure it fits the style of operations.

E.g., a hotel with 2 restaurants, a lobby bar, a cocktail bar, a rooftop lounge and 2 kitchens would need a system more complex, with transfers between outlets and storage units.

E.g., a coffee house with 20 seats, could make do with the use a more simplified monitoring system.

All cost controlling does, is keep track of the usage of our goods (ingredients). We do not have to invest in expensive software, a simple spreadsheet will go a long way. Basic information retrieved from sales reports should be available of course, without it, it would not be possible.

Controlling our costs can be done on several levels. We might opt to only have information per day or per week, or we might want to have information that is more specific during the day.

E.g., breakfast, lunch, dinner, late night party, etc.

This might be useful if we want to understand how well a party was managed or how efficient a specific service was.

As we can see in the examples below, we can even determine how well we manage things per dish or food group. This allows us to compare for instance fish main courses to meat main courses.

E.g., soups, appetizers, main courses, desserts, 5 course menus, etc.

Using the system on a day-to-day basis allows us to find errors and opportunities per day. This could be useful if we want to understand how Mondays compare to Tuesdays for instance. It should be clear there is a lot of freedom to how we want to apply the control systems in our restaurant. For most hospitality businesses, food and drinks are the main money makers. The more control we have over everything the better we can minimize costs and maximizing profits.

Food cost or beverage cost is a tool that will indicate the relationship between the costs of the food/beverage usage in comparison to the turnover created. The lower the food- or beverage cost, the better. Increasing profit will always be based on two fundamental things. On the one hand we should try to reduce costs, in this case the food cost and the beverage cost, and on the other hand we should find ways to increase the revenues, which can be done by optimizing our menu, the table and seating mix, following up on forecasts and more.

E.g., if the cost of 1 kg tomatoes is €1, can we buy it for €0,99?

E.g., if the price on the menu for a drink is €2, can we sell it for €2,01?

These are questions we need to ask every day and try to strike a balance between lowering costs, increasing revenue and keeping sales stable (or increase sales). Losing sales does not necessarily lead to a lower gross profit.

Cost	Revenue	Sales	C. totals	R. totals	Gross profit
€ 1,00	€ 2,00	100	€ 100,00	€ 200,00	€ 100,00
€ 0,99	€ 2,00	100	€ 99,00	€ 200,00	€ 101,00
€ 1,00	€ 2,01	100	€ 100,00	€ 201,00	€ 101,00
€ 0,99	€ 2,01	100	€ 99,00	€ 201,00	€ 102,00
€ 1,00	€ 2,01	99	€ 99,00	€ 198,99	€ 99,99
€ 0,99	€ 2,01	99	€ 98,01	€ 198,99	€ 100,98
€ 1,00	€ 2,50	75	€ 75,00	€ 187,50	€ 112,50

Figure 12: the relationship between sales price and sales numbers.

In the figure above we an example of scenarios of what the impact could be on the gross profit if the cost would decrease and/or sales price (revenue) would decrease or increase. As we can see, losing sales (customers) does not always lead to a lower gross profit, however we should try to avoid it.

The principle of COGS

To understand how food- and beverage cost is calculated, we must first understand the principle of COGS (cost of goods sold). When dealing with food, the COGS are food ingredients, when dealing with beverages the COGS are beverage ingredients.

The cost of goods sold, is all costs (products, time, labor, energy, marketing, etc.) that are required to make or produce 1 good(s). In this case a drink or a meal. However, there are many ways to go about this. We can figure out for instance what the cost of electricity or insurance would be per meal sold. We would need to apply cost accounting techniques, but to keep it manageable and practical we will stick with the ingredient costs.

When food is used in beverages (cocktails, smoothies, etc.) or when beverage is used to cook (white wine sauce, etc.) the monetary value is deducted from one side and added to the other side, to balance everything out. To make sure food items do not end up in beverage costs and vice versa. This ensures that the right COGS is applied.

E.g., the bartender uses 5 kg strawberries (€25) to mix cocktails (€125). This would mean the inventory of food decreases (higher usage, therefore the total cost of food ingredients increases). But it was not used for food production. This also means that there is no food revenue for these strawberries (there is beverage revenue however).

We can understand that the bartender is quite pleased. He gets 'free' ingredients and therefore has no costs and in return generates €125 in revenue. Therefor his revenue equals gross profit. The kitchen chef will be much less pleased. His food usage goes up by €25 and he receives no revenue for it. To correct this, the cost of food (-€25 strawberries) would be deducted from the total purchasing costs of food and be transferred to the purchasing costs of the bar (+€25 cost of beverage, strawberries). Doing so will ensure that costs are always linked to the correct cost item.

	Kitchen		Bar	
	Ingredient costs	Food revenue	Ingredient costs	Beverage revenue
	€ 500,00	€ 2.500,00	€ 500,00	€ 2.000,00
Strawberries	€ 25,00	€ -	€ -	€ 125,00
Total	€ 525,00	€ 2.500,00	€ 500,00	€ 2.125,00
Cost percentage	21,00%		23,53%	
	€ 500,00	€ 2.500,00	€ 500,00	€ 2.000,00
Strawberries	€ 25,00	€ -	€ -	€ 125,00
Strawberries	€ -25,00		€ 25,00	
Total	€ 500,00	€ 2.500,00	€ 525,00	€ 2.125,00
Cost percentage	20,00%		24,71%	

Figure 13: the overview of the transfers between food cost and beverage cost.

As we can see in the figure above, if the cost of the strawberries is not transferred from the kitchen (food) to the bar (beverage) the food cost will increase from 20% to 21% and beverage cost will drop from 24,71% to 23,53%. After the transfer has taken place, the food cost and beverage cost are now correct (20% and 24,71%).

E.g., if we buy 1 kg tomatoes to make a soup for €1,50 and this serves 3 persons. The cost of goods sold is €0,50. We always convert to a single serving/person/pax (unit(s) per person).

Once the COGS is calculated we can calculate the food- and beverage cost.

Food cost ≠ cost of food

Beverage cost ≠ cost of beverage

Cost of food and cost of beverage are the costs expressed in value (money) and the food cost and the beverage cost are these values expressed in a percentage in relation to the revenue that was generated.

You can calculate the food cost and beverage cost with the formulas below.

(Net cost of food (COGS) / net sales price) x 100 = food cost

(Net cost of beverage / net sales price) x 100 = beverage cost

The formulas above can be used to calculate the cost percentage per item. To calculate the food- or beverage cost in terms of actual sales we would use the same formula however slightly different.

(Total net cost of food / net food revenue) x 100 = food cost

(Total net cost of beverage / net beverage revenue) x 100 = beverage cost

E.g., we have a dish that we sell for €10 (net price), and it costs €2,50 (net price) to make. The food cost would be 25% ((2,5 / 10) x 100).

E.g., we have sold 100 beers (1 beer sells @ €1) for a total revenue of €100. 1 Beer costs €0,20. The total cost would be €20 (€0,20 x 100). This would result in a beverage cost of 20% ((20 / 100) x 100).

When we have a food cost of 25% it means that for every €100 revenue (net) we spend €25 on ingredients.

Costs of labor

The other direct 'variable' cost that we could use to determine the COGS for a food- or beverage item on the menu would be labor costs or wages. Costs always take a substantial chunk out of our profit. Wages in the restaurant industry are usually around 30%, but it could be much higher depending on the level of service. Costs of labor have a direct impact on the profit margins per item we sell.

Direct wages like that of kitchen staff and bartenders for instance are easy to add up to the cost of goods sold. Because these people are directly responsible for the production of food items and beverage items, we can determine what the production of 1 item costs in terms of wages for the person responsible producing it. Wages like that of waiters, cleaning staff, managers and so on can also be incorporated but that is more complex, also they are not directly involved in the production of an item.

Based on, preparation time, which we can link to the menu item sheet, we can figure out what the cost of labor is per unit produced. Usually, we only keep track of food cost and beverage cost in terms of production cost. However, if we want to have a better understanding of what is happening in our restaurant then this is an essential indicator to keep track of.

The labor cost is a key tool that indicates the relationship between the cost of labor in comparison to the turnover created.

Labor cost ≠ cost of labor.

E.g., in our restaurant are working 2 kitchen chefs, 3 waiters and 1 manager for a total salary cost of €12.650 per month. We have sold 1.500 items, then that means that each item costs €8,43 in wages (€12.650 / 1500). We have a revenue of €37.500 in total, which would mean that salary costs in our restaurant are 33,73% ((€12.650 / €37.500) x 100).

As we can see in the example above, it is simple to calculate the cost of labor per item. However, in terms of production we do not know if we are doing a decent job or not. We can use labor cost variance analyses to figure out how labor have impacted our results.

Implementing a cost control system

In most cases we already have some sort of control system that we use.

E.g., when to order, how much to order, forecasting revenue, etc.

How simplistic as it may seem, it is a form of control and monitoring. To optimize or start with a system we need to figure out what it is we want to get out of the system.

Setting up a useful cost control system can be a time-consuming thing. However, once the system is in place it will assist us in increasing profits. This system also needs constant monitoring and updating for it to be efficient. In most cases only a few people are actively involved in overseeing this system.

E.g., chef, bartender, manager, restaurant manager, etc.

In much larger hospitality businesses, even more people will be directly involved in this system.

E.g., storekeeper, purchase manager, the chef, accounting, banqueting, maître d' hotel, food & beverage manager, district manager, etc.

When we say involved, we mean people who manage input of data and assist in analyzing the results and taking action. Everyone is involved to a degree. A waiter who keeps spilling bottles of wine for instance, is actively involved in increasing the beverage cost.

To optimize our gross profit, the first thing we need to do, is start monitoring the costs of food and the costs of beverage. In other words, the ingredients costs. We need to make sure a few other things are in place as well.

- *Menu item sheets (MIS).*
- *Purchasing and receiving.*
- *Inventory management.*
- *Usage and waste by staff.*
- *Menu engineering.*
- *Training of staff.*

Good individual systems of the above-mentioned elements are important when it comes to optimizing cost control and therefore will help to optimize our gross operating profit (GOP) or contribution margins. Of course, everything we do has an influence on profits, costs, guest satisfaction, service, etc. and obviously there is more than just these elements to manage. But if we can make sure these elements run smoothly, we can rest assured that our restaurant will benefit from it.

Menu item sheets

To start with food- and beverage cost control we need to have menu item sheets (MIS) in place. Without it, there is no way we can get started. The MIS is a standardization of the production and presentation of a certain meal or beverage. It has all the information about said meal/drink (prices, sales price, food cost, photo, recipe, preparation time, yield, etc.). Everything we need to know about this item. A menu item sheet is more than just a recipe. The recipe is the basis, however.

A rule when creating menu item sheets is that we must be specific about the recipe. We do not measure in cups, spoons, drops, pinches etc. We always measure in grams, ounces, liters, gallons and so on. The reason for this, is to avoid our standard being different every time (so not being as standard as it should be).

E.g., we measure 1 cup, our colleague measures 1 cup (but a larger cup). Already there are different amounts of ingredients. The same goes, for flat and heaped spoons. However, 1 ounce will always be 1 ounce. And a liter will always be a liter. There is no way to misinterpreted this.

E.g., let us say we have only 1 meal and we make this meal 50 times in a week. And half of time we measure wrong by 1 gram too much (we measure by feeling). That is 25 grams a week or 1.300 grams in a year (25 x 52). We can imagine the 'extra' unnecessary costs we would make during a year with multiple meals. It would be a lot. Especially, if it is an expensive ingredient like saffron @ €15 per gram. We will calculate variance analyses tot figure to what extend this is a problem and what it is costing us.

Menu item sheets are made per dish/drink. If we have 10 dishes, we will have 10 menu item sheets. When it comes to beverages, we should have MIS for drinks that need to be prepared and have multiple ingredients (cocktails, smoothies, etc.).

For some recipes it is quite useful to perform a yield test. This will be explained later. When doing a yield test, make sure it is attached to the MIS. It will come in handy when making a planning, serving groups, and placing purchase orders with your suppliers.

By implementing MIS, we create a standard. It means, 'this dish should always be made like this.' In theory there is no room for adjustments, if this MIS is in place, it must be respected. Making on the fly changes and not respecting the standard we set, goes against the whole concept of cost control. We should not be afraid it will leave us with no room for creativity to make 'specials' and such. That is not the case. Specials are an exception to the rule. And while we could make a MIS for these items, a simple cost price analysis will do fine, most of the time. If all the menu item sheets are made, we should have a much better understanding of the items we offer to guests and the menu in general. Menu item sheets are the foundation for food- and beverage cost control. Once MIS are in place, we know exactly how much costs we should make per item, and we can budget and compare it to the results. Without MIS, we have no basis or guideline to fall back on.

Not only does it help us with the cost control, but it also has more advantages.

- *Every dish will be same every time (guests can expect the same dish every time they order it).*

- *It helps to set a sales price.*

- *It simplifies purchasing. Everybody should be able to purchase ingredients.*

- *It helps to minimize inventory size (no more questionable products in the inventory).*

- *It helps to calculate labor costs based on preparation time needed.*

- *Training of staff will be easier, (everybody should be able to make a certain dish with the same outcome). Less guidance and coaching are needed.*

- *New staff members can work more efficient from the start.*

- *If done right, the MIS should provide the most efficient way of preparing a dish or drink.*

- *The MIS gives insight in the composition of a dish or drink (diets for certain guests).*

- *It helps to simplify the H.A.C.P.P. (hazard analysis critical control points).*

Menu Item Sheet number	112							
Date	1-1-2014		Beverage type	Cocktail	Yield		x	
Name	Tropical Gold		Fbc%	22%				
Cost type	Beverage		Pbc%	48%				
Number of servings (recipe)	1		Recipe	Yes				
Ingredient	Amount	G. price	Packaging	Vat	N. price per ml		N. price	
Rum	30ml	18,99	750ml	20%	€	0,02	€	0,63
Creme de bananas	150ml	11,99	540ml	20%	€	0,02	€	2,78
Orange juice	30ml	2,84	1000ml	5%	€	0,00	€	0,08
					Cost of beverage		€	3,49
					Correction servings			1,00
					Cost of beverage		€	3,49
					Risk margin			4%
					Cost of beverage		€	3,63
					Fbc%			22%
		Photo			N. potential s. price		€	16,50
					Multiplier (vat 20%)			1,2
					G. potential s. price		€	19,80
					Sales price (menu)		€	9,00
					Net sales price		€	7,50
					Potential beverage cost			48%
Preparation and serving								
Step 1								
Step 2								
Step 3								
Step n								

Figure 14: the menu item sheet.

In the figure above we see an example of what a menu item sheet for a cocktail could look like. When making a MIS, we decide what information needs to be on this document. We could for example specify what glass needs to be used, how many ice cubes, or crushed ice, from which supplier what ingredient comes, and so on. We can be as elaborate as we want. Whatever we choose, we should make sure the basic info is most certainly printed on this document.

Purchasing and receiving

To control the costs of food and beverage it is important that we buy the right quality products for the right price at the right moment. Buying high quality products will result in longer shelf life, thus in less waste. It will increase the quality of a dish (resulting in a higher customer satisfaction). Purchasing products of lesser quality is never a satisfactory solution. If quality products result in too high a cost price, or in menu prices too expensive to sell. We should not purchase products of lesser quality, instead, we would manage portion sizes and optimize the menu, or if all fails, remove the dish from the menu.

When we buy products, we should always try to negotiate the lowest price possible. It will result in higher profits. Keep in mind that if we want the highest quality, we will pay the highest price. We cannot buy the best products at the lowest prices. When negotiating, do not negotiate just price, talk about the whole package. Maybe, we should accept a higher price if this means the supplier will help us in times of need (a special delivery even when they are closed, delivery late at night, better payment conditions and more). It is this type of service that will make a significant difference and has a positive impact on our business. A business deal should benefit both parties. Make sure you get a good deal, but always remember, it should be a win-win situation. When negotiating, make sure you do your homework. If we do not have the right information, we will not be able to get good deals. This way we have some ammo in the form of arguments as to why we should get a certain deal from a supplier. Also find multiple suppliers and try to start a bidding war. Most of the time, we instantly prefer a certain vendor. Confront suppliers with better offers gained from their competitors and see if they can at least match the offer.

E.g., if we need to negotiate prices for steaks. We should get all the information there is about the steak market. We should know our own figures (how much do we sell, what can we offer in terms of buying quantity and fast payment, etc.).

If we are not in touch with a certain market and do not have the time to do enough research. We can always ask someone who does have a good understanding of a specific market to assist in the negotiation process. It will make a substantial difference.

When purchasing products (and when negotiating), we should be specific. Not all tomatoes are the same, salmon is not just salmon, cheese it not just cheese, coffee is not just coffee… Ordering a product with certain specifications, will make sure we always get the same result. It would be wise to make a product specification list. This way we always get exactly what we have asked for. Of course, on our MIS we are specific when it comes to the ingredients.

E.g., we need to make apple cakes. Let us say we need 100 kg of apples. If we made a MIS based on large apples (Jonagold, 95 mm) and now we buy whatever type of apple (let us say we get smaller ones, Elstar, 65 mm). We will have more product waste (more apple cores), thus less yield. We would need more apples.

E.g., let us say we are still baking apple cakes and the MIS was based on sweet apples (Jonagold), and now we make these cakes with sour apples (Granny Smith). We will not have the same apple cake in the end.

As made clear in the previous examples, we could get in serious trouble with our customers, but also on an operational level.

There is only one way to order from suppliers. And that is by specifying our purchase orders as detailed as need be. This also makes sure there is no discussion when the requirements were not met at delivery.

Product	Apple		Product	Coffee
Type	Granny Smith		Type	100% Arabica
Size	60-70		Brand	Brand X
Color	Green		Content	Beans
Origine	France		Size	1Kg bags
Class	1		Color	No
Brix			Origine	Brazil
Packaging	Box of 50 pcs		Class	1
Quality remarks	No mould, no brown soft spots		Brix	No
Certification	No		Packaging	Box of 10x bags 1Kg
			Quality remarks	Dry, fresh coffee smell
			Certification	Rainforest Alliance Fairtrade

Figure 15: the specifications of a purchase order.

*Brix is the sweetness of a product. It is mostly used for fruit that has a lot of juice (melons, oranges, pineapples, etc.) Brix is measured with a brix meter device. It is an excellent indicator to assess products on sweetness.

In the previous figure we can see how we could send out our specifications. We can make it as elaborated as we want. Use product specifications to check if the delivered goods meet the requirements. For certain products, like fish, we would need to have it delivered at certain temperatures. This is not just a specification, but it is also good practice of H.A.C.C.P.

If products do not meet the agreed specifications, we do not accept the products, or we accept them under specific terms. If products do not meet the hygienic or food safety standards, we must always refuse the products. Accepting inferior quality, accepting the wrong quantity, accepting the wrong price... due to a bad purchasing and receiving management will cost a lot of money. Purchasing should be done according to forecasts.

We should also consider the seasons. Normally we should already do this by updating and changing the menu on a regular basis. We should keep in mind that if we do not, we might be serving summer dishes in the winter, and purchasing ingredients at premium prices due to low availability, import or even receiving much lesser quality.

E.g., serving strawberries in the winter which are more expensive and of lesser quality.

Inventory management

When we buy ingredients is it necessary to store these in the most optimal conditions (especially with products that spoil fast). Not doing so will result in waste (losing money), and/or serving customers products of lesser quality. This could result in unsatisfied, non-returning customers (losing money).

An inventory should be organized and clean (resulting in a more accurate inventory count). The trick is to always have just enough of everything. This avoids 'no-sales,' avoids having money tied up in stock and improve stock rotation.

A good inventory should have just enough of everything, and the last item should leave the moment the new/fresh products are being delivered. This means we need to account for enough ingredients to stay operational and cover for the delivery time of new products. Fortunately for our industry this is never really a problem since we usually get fresh deliveries ever day or every other day.

E.g., we use 15 kg of tomatoes per day. We should have 15 kg of tomatoes in stock every day. Keep in mind the delivery time. Let us say the supplier can only deliver once every 2 days. This means we need to order for two days every time we order. If not, we had run out of tomatoes on the second day. We might have to account for specific days to have more stock on hand. For instance, if we know on Fridays, we sell double the amount of tomato soups.

E.g., we calculate that at any given moment we should have 10 kg of oranges (to make fresh orange juice). This might be the case for wintertime. However, in the summertime we could be off. So, keep this in mind. This works in the opposite direction as well.

To keep a good inventory set an iron inventory (this is the amount that should always be on hand). Setting the bare minimum in stock can be done by keeping track of the usage per day, week, and month. This way we can find out what we need daily.

E.g., if we need 5 kg broccoli per day, we have no need to buy 35 kg on Monday to last for the whole week. Buying 5 kg per day is more sensible. This also optimizes the freshness of the products.

Depending on the products, sometimes it is just not possible to have delivery every day. For products like potatoes there is no need to have these delivered every day. Once or twice a week is fine. This of course is different for every product.

Also be sure to set a maximum. When we have more than we need, this 'surplus' will result in stock rotation becoming slow and we will have to throw away products. Setting the maximum can be calculated based on the busy moments and setting some risk margins. So, we can set different minimums and maximums for each time of the year, month, or week, depending on the historical data. The key to having an optimized inventory is planning and checking previous periods.

Since the inventory will tell us at the end of the month, how much is used. It is important to keep track of everything that comes in and everything that leaves the inventory. If we lose track of where, when, what products were being used we will end up with a lot of 'missing' items. On top of that it will affect the costs in a negative way. Depending on the business, we should keep written records of transfers (value that should either be credited or debited to food- or beverage cost), store requisition sheets, waste reports and so on.

E.g., the marketing department wants to donate 100 steaks to a homeless shelter. This is a cost of food with no revenue in return. Thus, raising the food cost. This, however, would be a transfer taken out of the food cost. In other words, this cost should be paid by the marketing department. This would raise the marketing cost but does not affect the food cost at all.

E.g., the kitchen uses wine to make a sauce. This is a beverage used as food. This would mean the following. Beverage should be credited for the price of the used amount of wine, and food should be debited for the price of the wine. This ensures usage is always linked to the right type of cost. This works the other way around as well, as previously discussed.

Using store requests (within larger companies) keeps evidence on paper, of what happened to which product when the storekeeper is not available and access to the inventory was granted by management. The person taking goods from the inventory must write this down in an inventory booklet.

Usage and waste

It is important that staff members, be it in the kitchen, be it in the bar use products with the necessary respect, not doing so will result in higher waste. Also, they must respect the menu item sheets, failing to respect the MIS will cost money.

E.g., let us say we sell only 1 product, steak. We serve 200 g steak for €15 (net) on the menu. Let us see what happens if we fail to respect the MIS. We serve 10 g more per steak because we cut steaks by feeling. This might seem like it is not a big deal. However, it is important.

	MIS	Actual
Price per Kg	€ 25,00	€ 25,00
Portion size Kg	0,200	0,210
Sold	100	100
Revenue	€ 1.500,00	€ 1.500,00
Cost of food	€ 500,00	€ 525,00
Food cost	33%	35%

Figure 16: the comparison between cost of food and actual usage.

In the figure above we can see what happens if we were to serve 10 g more than the standard. It raises the food cost with 2%. Over a total of 100 steaks sold, we used 1 kg more than we were supposed to use. Not respecting the standardizations will cost a lot of money.

The same thing applies to waste. If we throw away more than we are supposed to, we will need to buy additional ingredients, and the food cost and/or beverage cost will go up.

Keeping track of waste/spillage (spilling wine, cutting potatoes to rough… or because products spoiled due to lack of proper purchasing, receiving, and storing) in all parts of the restaurant is important. This will help to clarify what caused the loss of money. And it gives us a chance to make the necessary adjustments.

	Apples	Apples
Costs	€ 300,00	€ 300,00
Used	€ 200,00	€ 200,00
Waste	€ 15,00	€ -
Spoiled	€ 15,00	€ -
Usage	€ 230,00	€ 200,00
Revenue	€ 600,00	€ 600,00
Food cost	38,33%	33,33%

Figure 17: the impact of waste and spoilage on usage.

In the figure above we can see that the food cost increased by 5% because we wasted (dropped some apples on the ground, accidentally threw some away and peeled some to rough) some of the apples. And because there was not a proper inventory system in place, we did not notice the apples that were stored in a corner of the refrigerator and went bad (spoiled goods). Notice the importance of taking care and storing products.

A special 'tool' was developed to track how much waste per product is allowed. It is called the yield test.

Menu engineering

Menu engineering is a term for optimizing the menu. Doing so will result in a better mix of dishes and drinks on the menu, higher net profits and more overall sales when done effectively. Having a good understanding of the menu creates opportunities.

Training of staff

Having well trained staff at right place will do wonders for our restaurant. Front of house staff needs to know how to sell/push certain items on the menu (raising profits) and how to manage products to avoid waste and spillage.

E.g., let us say we have 2 dishes on the menu. One has a food cost of 35% and one has a food cost of 25%. In this case, customers order a lot of item 1 (35%) and only a few ordered item 2 (25%). The average food cost will go up for every item 1 sold. The food cost will go down for every item number 2 sold.

	Sold	Price		Cost of food		Revenue		Cost total	Food cost
Item 1	200	€ 10,00	€	3,50	€	2.000,00	€	700,00	
Item 2	50	€ 12,00	€	3,00	€	600,00	€	150,00	
Total	250				€	2.600,00	€	850,00	33%
Item 1	150	€ 10,00	€	3,50	€	1.500,00	€	525,00	
Item 2	100	€ 12,00	€	3,00	€	1.200,00	€	300,00	
Total	250				€	2.700,00	€	825,00	31%

Figure 18: the impact of pushing specific items on the menu on the food cost.

The figure above is divided in two parts. The upper half shows us the food cost if we sold a lot more of item 1. In the lower half we see what happens if we follow up sales every hour during the service hours. When too much of item 1 is being sold we should tell staff to push item number 2 more. As a result, food cost was only 31% instead of 33% (we did sell more of item 2 because staff promoted this item very well).

When pushing items on the menu, we need to push the right items. Items that will have us end up with more profit instead of just a lower food cost. A higher food cost is acceptable if in return we make more profit. This is where menu engineering comes in handy. Together with well trained staff it will ensure a more efficient way of selling items on the menu and raising profit.

Chapter 6
The food- and beverage costs

When designing new menu items, we always must figure out how much it is going to cost to produce. In the case of food and beverage, which means ingredients. Preferably we aim for a target food- and beverage cost that was set in advance to guide us and help keep our expenses under control. That also means if a dish or drink is more expensive to make, we need to ask a higher sales price to maintain the food- and beverage cost or accept a lower profit margin. When setting sales prices, we need to make sure we can justify these prices to our customers and that these are in line with our competitors. Simply said, it means that we are limited in our choices. We cannot ask for any price on the menu and sometimes that means we must accept a higher food- or beverage cost. There are many scenarios.

E.g., if we want to maintain a food cost of 20% to produce a tuna salad and it costs €5 to make, then we need to ask €25 (plus value added tax) on the menu. But what if customers aren't willing to pay this price? What should we do if every other restaurant in the area asks €17 for the same salad?

E.g., if the production cost would go up to €6, we would have to charge €30 and if the ingredient prices go down to €4, we could ask €20 for a salad.

As is made clear in the previous examples, while it is important to figure out what the food cost and beverage cost of the items are, we have limitations when it comes to price setting. We can take different actions to either justify the sales price, find a way to make production cheaper or accept a higher food cost. It all depends on the situation.

To calculate the food- and beverage cost we need to know what the revenue or sales price of an item is and what the cost of production is. There are 3 techniques we can use to find the cost of food and the cost of beverage.

The food- and beverage costs

In theory there are 4 types of food- and beverage costs.

Forecasted food- and beverage cost (pre-calculated based on historical data and expectations), we use this to set up the calculations.

Potential food- and beverage cost (pre-calculated, based on the actual price setting, this is the theoretical food- and beverage cost that should be always achieved). This will be the target (estimated/budgeted/forecasted/potential) food- and beverage cost.

Actual food- and beverage cost (calculated after a specific period and is the result of the actual sales and purchases.

Net food- and beverage cost (calculated on a day-to-day basis). Based on the direct purchases of the kitchen or bar and inventory movement to the kitchen or bar on a specific day. Most of the time spot checks are used on the more expensive items instead, because this can be overly complex, and takes up a lot of the time, we do not use it to manage the restaurant. When it comes to events and groups it gives a distorted view of what is going on and leads to misinterpretation of the data.

The forecasted food- and beverage cost is used to get an idea of the minimum sales price. After setting the sales price on the menu, the potential cost is calculated (this is the cost we should strive for and is compared to the actual cost after a specific period).

Opting for a food cost and beverage cost control on a day-to-day basis is fine (gives more control). However, do not make decisions based on daily presented food- and beverage costs. Make decisions on a monthly or weekly basis.

Cost-plus pricing

Cost-plus pricing or mark-up pricing is based on calculating all the ingredients needed to produce an item. It is the most accurate technique, but it is also very time consuming. Because we take all ingredients into consideration we are working with high accuracy, but due to the many changes in purchasing prices on a monthly, weekly, and even daily basis we must keep updating our system.

We will use an example to illustrate how cost-plus pricing works.

Let us say, we have 1 meal on the menu: steak with fries. To keep it simple, we assume that these are the only 2 ingredients, no mayonnaise, no salad on the side etc.

The menu item sheet tells us we must serve 200 g steak and 250 g fries per person.

The purchasing prices are €9,54 per kg steak and €5,30 per 10 kg fries. These prices are the gross purchasing prices (including 6% vat), this can be seen in column B. We find the net purchasing prices in column C.

A	B	C	D	E
Product	Purchasing price gross	Purchasing price net	Price per unit (Kg, L,..)	Recipe
Steak	€9,54 per 1Kg	€9,00 per 1Kg	€ 9,00	€ 1,80
Fries	€5,30 per 10Kg	€5,00 per 10Kg	€ 0,50	€ 0,13
Total				€ 1,93

To calculate the net price, we can use the following formula.

Gross purchasing price / (1 + (vat / 100)) = net purchasing price

€9,54 / (1 + (6 / 100)) =

€9,54 / (1 + 0,06) =

€9,54 / 1,06 = €9,00 net purchasing price

And

€5,30 / 1,06 = €5,00 net purchasing price

Once we have figured out what the net prices are we need to convert these prices to 1 single unit of measurement so we can use it to determine the ingredient cost for our meal. In this case we have fries that were purchased @ 10 kg per bag. This needs to be converted to the price per kg or 1.000 grams.

For menu item sheets, grams and milliliters are the preferred units of measurement if we are dealing with single servings. If we were to produce a multitude of the same dish (preparing large batches) for instance for an event of hundreds of people. Then we could have a separate specification on the menu item sheet for larger quantities, for instance per 100 servings.

In column D the prices are converted to 'per unit' (kg).

To find the cost price per unit we need to know the packaging sizes. In this case it is 10 kg per bag of fries.

We can use the following formula.

Net purchasing price / unit per packaging = purchase price per unit

€5,00 / 10 kg = €0,50 per kg or 1.000 g

From this point on it is straightforward to calculate the cost per ingredient for a dish and what the total cost price (cost of food) for a dish is. We simply multiply the cost price per unit by the amount that needs to be used according to the recipe.

Price per unit x units needed = cost of food

€9,00 x 0,2 kg = €1,80

And

€0,50 x 0,25 kg = €0,125 ≈ €0,13

The cost of food for our steak with fries would be €1,93 (€1,80 +€0,13).

This means for every meal that we sell; it costs €1,93 to make. If there were 100 dishes sold, it would cost €193 (100 x €1,93). Granted the purchasing prices do not change and the measurements are precise.

Prime-ingredient cost pricing

The prime-ingredient costing technique takes into consideration only the most expensive ingredient and/or the ingredient that makes up most of the dish or beverage.

For our restaurant with the example of the steak and fries, the steak represents 93,26% ((€1,80 / €1,93) x 100) of this dish in terms of cost. It is also the most expensive ingredient @ €9,00 per kg compared to the fries @ €0,50 per kg.

The steak is the most important ingredient in this dish. Meaning that changes in prices, waste, portion sizes, etc. will have a stronger impact on steak than on profit margins than fries.

Since we know that most of the cost goes towards the steak we could decide to not bother with the calculations of other ingredients. We only calculate the cost price for the steak (the prime-ingredient). While this is not the most accurate way of cost pricing, it is time efficient and an accurate estimation. In reality, setting a cost price based on the prime ingredient(s) is done very often. Especially when setting prices for daily or weekly specials. In most cases a chef does not have the time to perform all the calculations, but he or she will have a good understanding of what each ingredient costs.

Ingredient-approach pricing

The ingredient-approach pricing technique starts the same as the cost-plus pricing method. The difference is that we assume that if the price of the prime-ingredient changes, all ingredients change accordingly. In our example that would mean if the purchasing price of the steak would increase by 10%, we assume the purchasing price of fries increases by 10% as well (even if it does not).

The costing techniques compared

E.g., let us say the purchasing price of steak goes up with 10%. This would mean steak will now cost €1,98 (€1,80 x 1,1). The menu item sheet needs to be adjusted. In the figure below we see how each method provides a different new cost of food.

	MIS	New MIS	Calculation
Cost-plus	€ 1,93	€ 2,11	(€1,80 x 1,1) + €0,13
Prime	€ 1,80	€ 1,98	(€1,80 x 1,1)
Approach	€ 1,93	€ 2,12	(€1,80 x 1,1) + (€0,13 x 1,1)

Figure 20: the results of the different costing techniques.

Once all the costs of food and costs of beverages are calculated we can start setting prices on the menu.

The risk margins

To tackle small purchase price fluctuations and to save time recalculating costs with every change, we can use a risk margin. Depending on the ingredient, prices can vary from day to day or be fixed for longer periods. This depends on a lot of external factors. A risk margin between 1% and 5% is acceptable. We should avoid risk margins that are too high.

Risk margins increase the cost of food and the cost of beverage on paper, however if we set prices based on costs, we should be careful that risk margins do not force us to ask sales prices that are on the expensive side.

Chapter 7
The price setting

When setting prices, the cost of food and cost of beverage per item is a guideline. Do not neglect to use other price setting rules. We must check prices of the competition and figure out what guests are willing to pay. If restaurants in the area are pricing their spaghetti bolognaise for €10. We should not be asking €6, nor should we ask €30. No matter what the cost of food or beverage is. We must accept the fact that we must stay competitive. We need to balance costs, sales prices, and the willingness to pay from our guests. Understandably, we need to know the market.

Setting the net sales price

To set a price based on the cost of food or cost of beverage, we would need a forecast cost. This is a cost percentage based on historical data, forecasted sales, the market, etc. However, there are some general guidelines we can use.

We would like to have a food cost of 30% and a beverage cost of 20%. This can be divided into subcategories.

Food cost   *35%*

- Soups 10%
- Main   30 35%
- Dessert 25%
- Pastry 15%-25%

Beverage cost   *20%*

- Coffee and tea   5%
- Soft drinks   10%
- Smoothies   30%
- Wines   20-60%
- Cocktails   20-40%

Depending on the products and the price setting, in some cases we would have to accept a higher cost percentage. Wine will usually have a higher beverage cost than beer. Lobster, caviar, and other luxury foods will have higher food cost compared to tuna or tomatoes for instance. If the market is incredibly competitive this will cause sales prices to drop and costs percentages to rise, because we want to be able to compete.

In the example of the steak and fries the cost of food was €2,03. Let us set a sales price for this dish. It is a main course, therefore 35% is the forecasted food cost.

We can use the following formula to set a target sales price.

Cost of food / food cost percentage = target net sales price

€2,03 / 35% =

€2,03 / (35 / 100) =

€2,03 / 0,35 = €5,80

To find the gross profit margin of this dish we subtract the cost of food from the target net sales price. The profit margin of this dish is €3,77 (€5,80 – €2,03).

We have used the guideline of 35% in the previous part. However, let us say we would like to be more ambitious, and we want to strive for a lower cost percentage. Then, we could lower the percentage (from 35% to any other percentage). If we decided to lower to forecasted food cost to 29%, the target net sales price would be €7 (€2,03 / 0,29) and the profit margin would be €4,97 (€7 – €2,03) per dish.

Setting the gross sales price

Often, we do not really work with the setting of the net sales prices as previously discussed. We only do this is we are driven by the cost percentages. Most of the time we will figure out what the cost of food and the cost of beverage is and decide directly what the price on the menu should be. Because prices are often set based on the market and not based on the costs. The menu price or the gross sales price is the price customers are paying for the food and drinks in our restaurant.

The price on the menu has taxes included, normally speaking this would be value added tax (VAT). But it could also include service taxes if we pay staff based on the sales volume and more.

Setting the price on the menu can be done in two ways. We can start from the costs and determine how much we should be asking or work the other way around and start with the price we want to ask. To calculate the gross sales price (price on the menu) we can start with the net sales price and multiply this with all additional taxes and other percentages.

The formula we can use is the following.

Net sales price x ((1 + VAT %) x (1 + extra %) x (1 + extra %) ... = gross sales price

We could also first calculate the multiplier by using the following formula.

((1 + VAT %) x (1 + extra %) x (1 + extra %) … = multiplier

If we multiply the net sales prices with the multiplier, we also find the gross sales price.

Let us assume we only apply a VAT of 10%, then the multiplier would be 1,1 (1 + 10%). If we were to include a service tax or 5% the multiplier would be 1,15 ((1 + 10%) x (1 + 5%)) or 1,1 x 1,05 = 1,15.

To find the menu price we multiply the net sales price with the multiplier.

In previous part we decided the net sales price should be €7. The price on the menu would be €8,05 (€7 x 1,15).

As we said previously, often this is not the way to set prices on our menu. There are many factors that come into play in deciding the price on the menu. Let us assume for our example we aim at the higher segment of the market. We put this dish on the menu for €11. The moment we change this, every pre-calculation we have done so far does not apply anymore since we decided not to follow it (it would only apply if we asked €8,05 on the menu). The cost of food still applies but percentage wise it has gone up or down according to the price on the menu. This cost of food will now be used to calculate the potential or target food cost based on the actual menu price.

In this case the dish is sold for more than is necessary to maintain the target of 29% food cost, which was €8,05.

To calculate the net sales price, we use the following formula.

Gross sales price / multiplier = net sales price

€11 / 1,15 = €9,56 net sales price.

To find the potential food cost we use the standard food- and beverage cost formula.

(Net purchasing cost / net sales price) x 100 = food cost

(€2,03 / €9,56) x 100 = 21,23% food cost.

By putting a higher price on the menu, the potential food cost dropped from 29% to 21,23%.

In the figure below we can see the in the first column how it looks if we would set the prices based on the forecasted food cost of 35%. In the second column we can see what would happen if we changed the food cost from 35% to 29%. The last column shows us only the reverse calculation with the same multiplier and cost of food. We can see that the food cost now is indeed only 21% should we maintain a cost of food of €2,03.

	Forecast		Target			
Cost of food	€	2,03	€	2,03		
Food cost		35%		29%		
Net sales price	€	5,80	€	7,00		
Multiplier		1,15		1,15		
Menu price	€	6,67	€	8,05		
Menu price	€	6,67	€	8,05	€	11,00
Multiplier		1,15		1,15		1,15
Net sales price	€	5,80	€	7,00	€	9,57
Food cost		35%		29%		21%
Cost of food	€	2,03	€	2,03	€	2,03

Figure 21: the price setting based on the food cost.

E.g., we sell a red wine 'Merlot 2008', and we need to decide for what price we will put it on the menu. We purchase this wine for €6 per bottle and we sell it per glass and should achieve 20% beverage cost. Each bottle pours 6 glasses of wine.

Product		Merlot 2008	Calculation
Purchase price (gross)	€	6,00	
Vat		15%	
Net price	€	5,22	6 / 1,15
Number of glasses		6	
Net price per glass	€	0,87	5,22 / 6
Risk margin		2%	
Net price per glass (cost of beverage)	€	0,89	0,87 X 1,02
Forecast beverage cost		20%	
Required net sales price	€	4,43	0,89 / 0,2
Taxes		15%	Only the vat of 15%
Multiplier		1,15	1,15 X 1,00
Gross sales price per glass (menu)	€	5,10	4,43 X 1,15
Price on the menu (what we choose)	€	5,50	Decided keeping all aspects of pricing in mind
Potential net sales price per glass	€	4,78	5,50 / 1,15
Potential beverage cost		19%	(0,89 / 4,78) X 100

Figure 22: the complete price setting based on the market for wine.

In the previous figure we can see how the price setting can be done. Since this is a steady market a 2% risk margin is applied, this raises the cost of beverage by €0,02 (€0,87 x 2%). We then decide not to go with the advised menu price of €5,10 but to ask a higher price of €5,50 causing the net sale price to increase as well and the beverage cost to lower to 19%.

Monitoring the food- and beverage cost

To find out if we achieved the cost percentages we planned for, we need to compare the potential food- and beverage cost to the actual food- and beverage costs.

The example of steak and fries is used to demonstrate what steps to go through.

The sales price on the menu was €11 and the potential food cost was calculated at 21,23% or €2,03 cost of food. This is the budget, target, or potential food cost. This is what we can achieve should we do everything perfect. The first step is to calculate how much net revenue we have made. We can look at this per food item, per beverage item, per hour, per department and so on. In this case we assume we only sell 1 dish to keep it simple. The results are for one month.

We have sold 300 dishes. This should us a gross revenue of €3.300 (300 x €11) or €2.869,56 (€3.300 /1,15) net revenue. However, we have only managed to generate a net revenue of €2.695,65. Meaning that we have made less money than expected. So far it is clear that we are losing money on the revenue side. The difference in revenue can have many reasons.

E.g., discounts, complimentary meals, etc.

In the next step we compare the potential or target food cost with the actual food cost. This tells us whether we've have spent more, less or the exact amount of money on purchasing ingredients.

The potential cost of food is €609 (300 x €2,03). However, the actual cost of food is €700 after the inventory was accounted for. This could be due to certain factors as well. To understand clearer how the inventory has an impact we illustrate this with an example a bit further as well.

E.g., purchasing prices went up, the menu item sheet was not respected, waste, change in quality of ingredients, theft, etc.

To calculate the actual food- and beverage cost, we need to know how much we really used (this usage includes waste, spoilage, miscounts etc.). We must have a look at the inventory. The usage is calculated by using the following formula.

Starting inventory + purchases – closing inventory = usage

In this case the starting inventory was worth €500, there were purchases for €300 and the closing inventory was worth €100.

€500 + €300 – €100 = €700 usage (actual cost of food).

Once we know what the sales results and inventory results are we can start with the last step and figure how we did this month. We can use the standard food cost formula.

(Net cost of food or actual cost of food or usage / net revenue) x 100 = food cost

(€700 / €2.695,65) x 100 = 25,97%

Now we can compare the actual food- and beverage cost with the target costs.

The actual food cost is 25,97% and the potential food cost is 21,23%, which is an unfavorable difference of 4,74%.

In this case the target or estimated food cost according to the menu item sheet was not achieved and we did not achieve the revenue. In this example we are losing money on both sides. To find the difference of how much money was lost we use the following formula.

(Actual revenue – potential revenue) – (usage – potential cost of food) = difference

(€2695,65 – €2869,56) – (€700 – €609) = €173,91 – €91 = €264,91

In short, per dish served €0,88 is lost. (€264,91 / 300 sales).

Final food report month 1
Prices are net (no vat included)

Revenue	Forecast	Actual1
Food revenue	€ 187.445,00	€ 187.445,00
Allowances (discounts, etc…)		€ -5.874,00
Food revenue (w/o allowances)	€ 187.445,00	€ 181.571,00
Cost of food sold		
Opening inventory		€ 154.000,00
Food purchases		€ 94.256,00
Beverage to food for cooking		€ 20,00
Packaging to return (+)		*€ 20,00*
Packaging to return (-)		*€ -20,00*
Waste		€ 25,00
Closing inventory		€ -175.421,00
Gross cost of food (usage)	€ 61.245,00	€ 72.880,00
Credits to cost of food		
Marketing promotions		€ 236,00
Food to beverage for mixing		€ 50,00
Other credits (staff, management extra, etc…		€ 55,00
Total credits to cost of food		€ -341,00
Food cost		
Actual cost of food (usage)	€ 61.245,00	€ 72.539,00
Actual food cost	32,67%	39,95%

Figure 23: the final food report.

Final beverage report month 1
Prices are net (no vat included)

Revenue	Forecast	Actual1
Beverage revenue	€ 94.826,00	€ 94.826,00
Allowances (discounts, etc…)	€ -	€ -3.241,00
Beverage revenue (w/o allowances)	€ 94.826,00	€ 91.585,00
Cost of beverage sold		
Opening inventory		€ 11.215,00
Beverage purchases		€ 23.148,00
Food to beverage for mixing		€ 50,00
Packaging to return (+)		*€ 115,00*
Packaging to return (-)		*€ -115,00*
Waste (spillage)		€ 25,00
Closing inventory		€ -9.412,00
Gross cost of beverage (usage)	€ 24.456,00	€ 25.026,00
Credits to cost of beverage		
Marketing promotions (free drinks)		€ 236,00
Beverage to food for cooking		€ 20,00
Other credits (staff, management extra, etc…		€ 55,00
Total credits to cost of beverage		€ -311,00
Beverage cost		
Actual cost of beverage (usage)	€ 24.456,00	€ 24.715,00
Actual beverage cost	25,79%	26,99%

Figure 24: the final beverage report.

In the previous figures we can see an example of a beverage report and a food report. The numbers in the column 'forecast' are the values forecasted based on historical data. Based on the forecast and MIS, a food cost of 32,67% and a beverage cost of 25,79% was estimated. The actual cost percentages were not so good, as can be seen in the 'Actual1' column. There were some discounts (which we could and should consider when making a budget), that reduced the revenues.

Also, after the inventory count, there were differences. As we can also see, the bar used some food to prepare drinks (€50) and the kitchen used some beverages to cook (€20), this is credited and debited accordingly on both sides. Packaging that we received that needs to be returned to the supplier is normally a null operation. When packaging is lost it will increase the food- or beverage cost unless it is accounted for in a separate way, like a separate account for packaging.

Chapter 8
The beverage cost

Not much has been said about the beverage cost. That is because beverage cost follows the exact same steps and rules as food cost.

Important note: coffee and tea, however, are beverages when sold but usually are placed under revenue of food. Both are food items and are purchased as cost of food. Since we buy raw ingredients (coffee beans, tea leaves…) we must have these revenues and costs be accounted for the same cost type and revenue type. However sometimes it is placed under beverage. This is a decision we must make. Do not make the mistake of purchasing coffee beans (cost of food) and then sell it under beverage revenue. This will lead to an increase in food cost and decrease in beverage cost.

One advantage the beverage cost has over food cost is that the beverage market is quite stable and cost prices do not need regular updates.

E.g., the price of cola does not change every week, the price is the same during the year.

Beverage cost calculations are much more simplified than food cost calculation. This is because we purchase beverages per selling unit (1 can, 1 bottle…). If we buy 24 bottles of cola it means, we can serve 24 guests (24 servings) therefore we know instantly what the cost of beverage is.

For special drinks like cocktails, special coffees, etc. it would also be wise to have recipes worked out as a menu item sheets.

Prices for wine and liquor are also very stable since we would buy wine via a contract for x amount and get a fixed price. The prices will differ during the transition from wine year A to wine year B (even if it is the 'same wine'). The same applies for liquor.

High quality expensive wines and liquors can be charged at higher menu prices without a problem. Wines and liquors with a high stock rotation, like house wines should be kept at low purchasing prices. Sometimes it might be favorable to purchase wines at a discount price for a full year, while this might lead to lots of wine in stock it will not increase beverage cost due to monthly inventory.

	Month 1	Month 1	Month 2
Begin inventory	€ 500,00	€ 500,00	€ 11.250,00
Purchases	€ 1.000,00	€ 12.000,00	€ -
Closing inventory	€ 250,00	€ 11.250,00	€ 10.000,00
Usage	€ 1.250,00	€ 1.250,00	€ 1.250,00
Revenue	€ 6.250,00	€ 6.250,00	€ 6.250,00
Beverage cost	20,00%	20,00%	20,00%

Figure 25: the impact of monthly versus yearly purchases.

In the figure above we can see that it makes no difference whether we purchase wines every single month (1 x €1.000) or purchase wines for the entire year (12 x €1.000). The usage and the revenue stay the same, causing the beverage cost to stay the same as well. The only thing that is different is the closing inventory. In the second month (Month 2) we do not need to purchase house wines (if we have purchased for an entire year), this however does not lead to a cost of beverage of €0 or beverage cost of 0% due to inventory accounting. We did use wines with a value of €1.250 (sold) to sell @ €6.250 (revenue). The cost does not come from purchasing wines (which would have been the case if we bought @ €1.000 every month) but from taking/removing these items from the inventory (decreasing the stock which is an asset and turning it into a cost).

The upside which is not illustrated in this figure is that the beverage cost might decrease due to a discount for purchasing a large amount of wines for a full year.

Otherwise, there would not be a reason to purchase such a large quantity of wine. Instead of purchasing and receiving the wines, we could also opt to commit for a purchase of €12.000 but have it delivered every month and pay it every month on a call base (and still receive the discount because the supplier has a contractual agreement for these sales). This is however not the same as ordering a €1.000 worth of wine every month (since we can choose to order less or more), because in the example we are bound by contract.

When dealing with beverages, the dosage is particularly important. It is easy to spill expensive liquors. Therefor we should use bottle stoppers, to ensure bartenders will use the right amounts. A well-trained bartender is important. Do not let inexperienced staff pour expensive drinks. Do provide cross trainings and make sure everyone can pour at least the basic beverages.

The number of servings (glasses) we can pour out a bottle will depend on the portion size. For large groups that receive large discounts we can choose to pour 8 glasses out of a bottle instead of 6 for full prize paying customers.

E.g., full glass, half full, double, triple, etc.

Consignment

An interesting concept when dealing with the cost of beverage, is consignment. This means we receive the products, but we pay later, but only for the items we have sold. This allows us to have a higher stock and never running out (we don't have to pay for it) and also to have items in stock that are maybe too expensive, and we are not sure if we can sell these (we can have these in stock to test if customers are interested). Overall, there is a minimal risk. We do not have money tied up in inventory and this will increase cashflow significantly.

If we change the menu, we can just send all bottles back to the supplier (within a certain timeframe). After the monthly inventory count, we let the supplier know how many of which item we have sold, and the supplier will bill us only for the items that we have sold. This means we only must pay for what we sell. If we sell nothing, we do not have to pay. We do have to pay for spillage and waste of course (this is still our risk).

The consignment inventory is nothing special. It is just like the rest of the inventory. Except that, we let the supplier know how much we counted (and therefore used). Consignment is very low risk and interesting when selling more upscale type of drinks. However, it depends on the suppliers and whether they are willing to do business under a consignment contract.

The consignment products are part of the inventory when we count, but the goods are not our property. These still belong to the supplier. So, when we have a financially tough period and are low on cashflow, we could propose a consignment deal to better our financial position. Especially when, inventory turnover is slow, and we have a wide selection of wines.

We could consider buying inventory as pre-paid, and consignment as post-paid.

Inventory overview		
Inventory owned	€	1.000,00
Inventory in consignment	€	300,00
Total opening inventory	€	1.300,00
Purchases	€	200,00
Consignment received	€	60,00
Total purchased	€	260,00
Inventory owned total	€	1.200,00
Inventory in consignment total	€	360,00
Total inventory	€	1.560,00
Inventory owned closing	€	450,00
Inventory in consigment closing	€	150,00
Total closing inventory	€	600,00
Usage owned	€	750,00
Usage in consignment	€	210,00
Total usage	€	960,00

Figure 26: the consignment inventory overview.

In the figure above, the restaurant would receive an invoice from their supplier for €210. The other invoice of €200 (purchases) has already been received and/or paid.

The calculation of the beverage cost

E.g., for a wine 'red Merlot 2008' we received an overview of the sales numbers. In one month, we sold 425 glasses and had a turnover of €2.050 (gross). We have a potential beverage cost of 19% and we sell a glass of wine @ €5,50. Sales tax is 15%. We serve 6 glasses of wine out of one bottle.

In the figure below we can see how the beverage cost and the sales price of glass of wine have been calculated. We have calculated for a glass of wine, starting from a bottle of wine. We included a risk margin (in case of unexpected price increases) and decided on the sales price keeping in mind all aspects of price setting (in this case the menu prices of the competition).

Product	Red wine 'Merlot 2008'	Calculation
Purchase price	€ 6,00	
Vat	15%	
Net price	€ 5,22	6 / 1,15
Number of glasses	6	
Net price per glass	€ 0,87	5,22 / 6
Risk margin	2%	
Net price per glass (cost of beverage)	€ 0,89	0,87 X 1,02
Forecast beverage cost	20%	
Required net sales price	€ 4,43	0,89 / 0,2
Vat	15%	
Multiplier	1,15	1,15 X 1,00
Gross sales price per glass	€ 5,10	4,43 X 1,15
Price on the menu	€ 5,50	Decided keeping all aspects of pricing in mind
Potential net sales price per glass	€ 4,78	5,50 / 1,15
Potential beverage cost	19%	(0,89 / 4,78) X 100

Figure 27: the price setting for wine.

The beverage cost we should have according to the standard is 19%. This means the actual value of the cost of beverage should be €338,70 (19%). However, the actual revenue should have been €2.337,50 (425 x €5,50). In this case we have earned €287,50 less than we should've according to the MIS (€2.337,50 – €2.050,00).

Red wine Merlot 2008	Forecast (MIS)	Calculation MIS
Sold items (glasses)	425	
Gross revenue	€ 2.050,00	Sales report
Net revenue	€ 1.782,61	2050 / 1,15
Forecasted usage	€ 338,70	1782,61 x 0,19
Beverage cost	19%	(338,70 / 1782,61) x 100

Figure 28: the price setting for wine, the short overview.

Red wine Merlot 2008	Actual	Calculation actual
Sold items (glasses)	425	
Gross revenue	€ 2.050,00	Sales report
Net revenue	€ 1.782,61	2050 / 1,15
Opening inventory	€ 261,00	Check up
Purchases	€ 156,60	Invoices
Total inventory	€ 417,60	261 + 156,60
Closing inventory	€ 35,00	Check up
Inventory usage	€ 382,60	417,60 - 35
Beverage cost	21,46%	(382,60 / 1782,61) x 100

Figure 29: the comparison of the actual results with the budget.

In the figure above we can see what the actual beverage cost is. Not only was the wine sold for less than forecasted. But also, more wine was used than should have been used, €382,60 actual versus €378,25 according to the MIS (425 x €0,89). This €0,89 is the actual cost of 19% + a risk margin of 2% (€0,87 x 1,02).

Important when counting the beverage inventory is that we must count bottles and not glasses or servings (however we could do so if we want to). Let us assume we start with an inventory of 50 bottles of red wine Merlot 2008 or 300 (50 x 6) glasses/servings, which represents €261 (purchasing value or cost). When counting opened bottles, we must guess. This can be done really accurate. Most of the time a 'tenth' system is used or in other words a percentage. A full bottle is 10/10 (100%), half a bottle is 5/10 (50%) and so on. This percentage is multiplied with the cost price.

E.g., we count 2/10 of a bottle of tequila. This means the bottle holds about 20%. The cost price was €14,50 for a bottle. The value of the tequila left in the bottle is €2,90 (€14,50 x 20%).

In the example of our wine sales the difference in revenue could be due to giving discounts (giving a discount means, choosing to accept a loss in revenue which cannot be recuperated and lowers the profit margin and increases the beverage cost. The difference in inventory causes more of a problem. If there was spillage in any way, it should be found on the spillage report. Often, differences in inventory are caused by miscounting which happens due to poor inventory management.

Chapter 9
The yield test

When calculating cost of food and cost of beverage there is one thing that is important not to forget. When we buy a product, we would buy the product as it is, not the way it would be eaten or how customers would drink it. We must prepare food before it is served. And when preparing food, we must cut, slice, crop, trim and chop of bits and pieces. The result is an edible product, waste, and reusable waste. To find out how much we use and how much we would have to throw away, we must perform a yield test. The yield test tells us how much we use of the ingredient we bought. The product we purchase, we name this 'as purchased' (ap), we name the end product the edible product (ep).

The yield test is more commonly known as the butcher's test, since it is mostly done on meat, poultry, fish, etc. Because the test can be applied on numerous products (fruit, vegetables, meat, etc.), we call it a yield test instead. A yield test is mostly used on foods; however, it can be used to calculate the yield of drinks as well (smoothies).

Since even the same ingredients can vary in yield, we should do this test multiple times. Use the lowest yield percentage as the standard yield. There are 2 yield test methods.

1. Raw product pre-cooking method.
2. Post-cooking method.

It depends on the ingredients that we are testing. A product that would lose a lot of weight during cooking or baking should obviously be evaluated after cooking (mushrooms, tomatoes, etc.). A product that would lose a lot of weight from trimming, chopping, and cooking could be evaluated before (raw) and after cooking. Products that lose little weight during cooking can be assessed in raw state only.

We use the test that would give us the most realistic answer. The 'after cooking method' will obviously give you the most exact answer all the time. When we are preparing the food, we should respect preparation times. Overcooking will result in more weight loss for instance (lower yield).

To calculate the yield (percentage) we can use the formula below.

(Edible weight (ep) / weight as purchase (ap)) x 100 = yield

E.g., a whole chicken weights 2 kg when purchased. After preparation we have only 1 kg edible product left (minus bones, fat, etc.). The result is, 50% yield (1 kg / 2 kg) x 100.

Calculating the yield is important since it will tell us how much we are wasting (therefore raising the food cost), and it will help us figure out how much product we would need to produce a certain amount of dishes. When we buy an ingredient, we always purchase a certain amount of weight. But in most cases not all of it is useable (but we did pay for it). Think of bones and fat when purchasing meat, zest of citrus fruit, apple cores, etc. We are paying for waste.

E.g., let us say we buy a tenderloin, from which we would like to cut tournedos. We buy a piece of 4 kg @ €36,42 per kg. This would cost us €145,68 in total. This meat needs to be prepared (trimmed, sliced, etc.). We would like to know how much these costs.

	Weight	Price/Kg	Total price
As purchased	4000g	€ 36,42	€ 145,68
Fat (-)	300g	€ -	€ -
Bones (-)	300g	€ -	€ -
Usable trim (-)	900g	€ 8,45	€ -7,61
Other (-)	0g	€ -	€ -
Edible portion	2500g		€ 138,08
Yield %	63%	€ 55,23	
Cost multiplier		1,52	

Figure 30: the yield test.

After preparation we have 2,5 kg of clean meat left, 300 g of fat, 300 g bones and 900 g of reusable trim. The fat and bones in this case have no value (but we did pay for it, and we are throwing it away). The reusable trim (meat not usable for tournedos, but usable for other dishes) has a value of €8,45 per kg. Let us say we use this leftover meat to make a veal ragout. Normally we would buy the ragout meat at a certain price, this price is the value of the reusable trim (we can get prices from vendors, suppliers, etc. to get an estimate of what our waste is worth). We should always try to find ways to reuse the waste of an ingredient.

E.g., we can use waste like bones as a flavor maker in soup.

E.g., we can us waste to make daily specials.

To calculate the actual cost price for the tenderloin we can use the formula below.

((Total price – reusable product price) / edible portion in gram) x 1000 = actual price per kg

€145,68 – €0 fat – €0 bones – €7,61 reusable trim – €0 other = €138,07

(€138,07 / 2500 g) x 1000 = €55,23

The total value of usable trim is €7,61 (this would be a deduction to the total purchase price of €145,68) since this value is being used and not thrown away like the bones and fat. We have paid €145,68 for 2,5 kg of edible meat minus fat, bones, reusable trim and other. That means we paid €138,08 for 2,5 kg tenderloin (clean usable meat), instead of €91,05 (2,5 kg x €36,42).

Instead of €36,42 (€91,05 / 2,5 kg) per kg, we paid €55,23 (€138,08 / 2,5 kg) per kg. That is €18,81 per kg more (€55,23 – €36,42). In this case it is wise to buy pre-cut tournedos. If the price per kg for pre-cut is less than €55,23 per kg. The new calculated price per kg is the price we use to calculate costs and sales prices on the menu item sheet.

The yield for our example is 62,50% ((2.500 g / 4.000 g) x 100).

A yield of 62,50% means that we buy and pay for the full 100%, however we only can use 62,50% of the purchased weight (reusable trim not included, since we do not use it for this dish). We use 3.400 g, but only 2.500 g can be used for what the purchase was for in the first place.

To make it a little easier for future calculations we can use a multiplier. We can use this to calculate the cost of the usable weight per kg versus the purchase cost of the weight per kg. When the purchase price would change, we can use the multiplier to tell us the new actual price per kg instead of doing the test repeatedly. In this case the multiplier is 1,52 (€55,23 / €36,42).

We can use the following formula to calculate the multiplier.

Edible price per kg / as purchased price per kg = multiplier

If the purchase price would change to €38,50 per kg the new edible portion price per kg would be €58,52 (€38,50 x 1,52). We should understand how to use the yield test and the multiplier as it will give information on what the actual cost of food for an item is and allows for a better sales price setting.

Planning with the yield test

The yield test can help us plan and purchase more efficient. For most products, the yield is never 100%. If we know how much yield a certain product gives, we can calculate how much we need.

E.g., let us say we serve a group of guests. In total we would require 4 kg tournedos. We would not have enough if we purchased just the 4 kg tenderloin (since this is what we call 'dirty' meat, it is not prepared and not all of it is usable). We can use only 2,5 kg (62,5%). This would mean we would be 1,5 kg short in product.

To calculate how much of a certain product, we really need to order from our vendors we can use the following formula.

Edible product / yield = as purchased (weight to purchase)

E.g., let us say we need to serve 150 guests 200 g of tournedos each. Calculating 150 x 200 g = 30.000 g or 30 kg, would be wrong if we bought the meat 'dirty'. If we buy pre-cut tournedos, this would be accurate. In this case we do not have pre-cut and ordering 30 kg tenderloin would only give us 93 tournedos (30 kg x 62,5% = 18,75 kg or 18.750 g / 200 g = 93,75 ≈ 93 pieces). In this case, we would have a lot of unsatisfied guests.

If we would use yield to calculate the right amount, we would do much better. Every 200 g tournedos served is only 62,5% or the original ingredient. We divide the serving per guest by the yield, this gives us the amount we need to order per guest (200 g / 0,625 = 320 g)

We need to purchase 320 g of meat per guest. In total we would need to buy 48 kg of tenderloin (320 g x 150 = 48.000 / 1.000 = 48 kg). When preparing the products ourselves, we need to keep in mind that the product we buy, is not the same product we need. Based on the yield test we can make better decisions when it comes to planning and purchasing.

Chapter 10
Menu engineering

As a business we always try to reduce costs as much as possible on one side and increase revenue on the other side. By doing so we should be able to increase profits. Everything we do within the restaurant should be in service of generating more profit without harming the experiences of the guests. We have seen that we can increase profits by taking control of the costs of food and beverage.

The other side of profit optimization is selling more. That is why marketing is so important. However, there might be some things we might overlook, or have no idea of that it even exists.

One of those things would be the menu itself. We need as much information about the menu as possible to find out how well the restaurant is doing, and to find out what we can improve. The menu is one of the most important things that should convince customers to buy. We could even specifically steer customers to, what dish, what drink, we want them to buy. This concept is called menu engineering.

Apart from tweaking the menu, the setup of the restaurant needs to be optimized, waiting lines should be reduced and service cycle speed should be improved as well, just to name a few things.

To increase profit, we need to understand what the menu is doing and how to tweak it to optimize sales. Via menu engineering we can find out exactly what is going on. Adjusting the menu is necessary to manage the restaurant. Failing to do so, will cost a lot of money eventually.

By engineering the menu, we are going to look for the popular items with high profits margins. Because what we want on the menu, are popular, fast selling items that bring in lots of money. Menu engineering will help us to make better choices towards what we should and should not have on the menu. To start with menu engineering we need actual sales reports and menu item sheets, without it is impossible to even get started. Before we start, we must set some principles towards the menu.

The principles of the menu

It is important to have a consistent and balanced menu. To find out if we do, we use the principles of Omnes. These four principles will give us an idea of how well balanced the menu is. Keep in mind that every principle applies to a specific group of items (appetizers, main dishes, desserts, cocktails, etc.). Depending on the way the menu is divided we need to apply these principles per food- and beverage category. Do not apply the principles over the menu as a whole, this will not work.

Principle 1

The difference between the most expensive item of a product range and the cheapest item must be analyzed first to make sure the menu speaks to a specific clientele. The price range must be limited. The ratio between the most expensive and the least expensive product should not exceed 2,5-3. This is called the price range. The formula we can use is the following.

(Most expensive item / least expensive item) ≤ 2,5

Principle 2

The second principle aims to make sure the prices are homogeneous. To do so we must first calculate the price range. Then, divide it by 3 (because we set 3 price ranges usually: low, medium, and high). The number of items in the middle price range should at least be equal to the number of dishes in the highest and lowest price ranges. This ensures a good balance in the price ranges of the menu. This means that we have something for everyone. The formula we can use is the following one.

(Most expensive item – least expensive item) / 3 = Δ

The low segment will range from the lowest price to the lowest price + 1/3 of the difference between the most expensive item and the least expensive item (Δ). This would give the first segment a range of 25%.

The middle segment will range for 50%. By subtracting 1/3 from Δ, we will have the second and third segment which holds another 25%.

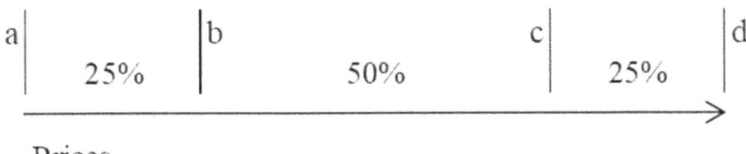

Prices

Figure 31: the prices range for the menu.

A = least expensive item

B = least expensive item + Δ

C = most expensive item – Δ

D = most expensive item

Most expensive item – least expensive item = Δ

Principle 3

This principle tells us if the menu is in line with customers' demands. It is the supply and demand ratio.

We can use the following formula.

Average price offered / average sales price = supply and demand ratio

To be able to calculate the above ratio we must first find the average sales of the product range (demand). And the average price of the items offered (offer). We use the formulas below to find the demand and offer.

Revenue / number of sold items = demand

Sum of the sales prices / number of items = offer

Once we know these numbers, we can calculate the supply and demand ratio and analyze the result.

Between 0,9 and 1 means that the ratio is good (the offer meets the demand).

Below 0,9 means that the prices on the menu are too high.

Above 1 means the prices are too low.

The prices we offer should always be a bit higher than the prices customers want to pay.

Principle 4

This principle tells us all about the promotions. When offering a complete course menu, it should be in line with the prices that customers would normally pay for the items individually. It should be always balanced, based on the average prices of the product ranges.

If the menu has a starter, a main and a dessert it should be priced accordingly. We can use the following formula to calculate a menu price.

Average price of item a + average price of item b + average price of item c + ...average price of item n = menu price

The pricing of the menu would be average price starter + average price main + average price dessert. Discounts can be applied of course, to generate more sales.

Always make sure the price setting is in range with the type of establishment.

The principles combined

E.g., the menu consists of 3 groups (starter, main and dessert). We only calculate everything for the desserts, to keep it simple. The lowest price is €14 and the highest is €26 for a dessert.

Principle 1

This would result in 1,85 (€26 / €14). This means the price setting between highest and lowest price is okay. If it would be lower, it would mean the gap between high and low is too big. Let us assume that we have a dessert of €84, then the result would be 6 (€84 / €14). It is obvious that the difference between the cheapest and most expensive dessert is too big.

Principle 2

Setting the product price segment ranges. $\Delta = €12$ (€26 – €14) / 3 = €4

The cheapest price range would be between €14 and €18 (€14 + €4).
The highest price range would be between €22 (€26 - €4) and €26.
The middle price range would be between €18 and €22.

Principle 3

There are 10 desserts on the menu with a total sum in sales prices of €204. The average offer price would be €20,40 (€204 / 10). Let us say we sold 850 desserts for a total €18.000 in revenue.

The average demanded price would be €21,18 (€18.000 / 850). The supply and demand ratio is 1,03 (€21,18 / €20,40). This means the menu is not homogenous and balanced. The offered prices do not meet the demanded prices. Since the ratio is above 1, it means that mostly high-priced desserts are being sold, and low-priced items are not sold enough. Our prices are too low for our customers because they are willing to spend more since we sell more of the expensive desserts.

Principle 4

Let us say we offer a promo menu of 1 starter, 1 main and 1 dessert. The price for this menu should be the average price of the starters (sum of starters' sales prices, divided by number of starters on the menu), the same goes for main and desserts. For desserts, the average would be €20,40. If we would add up the average of a main dish and the average of a starter, we will have the promo price.

Let us assume the total of this menu would be €95. To make it attractive we could give a discount of 10%. This will increase the number of sales. The menu is in line with the prices that we usually offer on our menu. If we deviate too much, people will wonder why the promo menu is so much cheaper compared to the normal menu and vice versa.

The classes

The point of analyzing the menu is to find out which items are doing well, and which items are not. To get a better understanding of what items on the menu represent what, in terms of popularity and profit margin we divide these into 4 classes: stars, workhorses, dogs, puzzles.

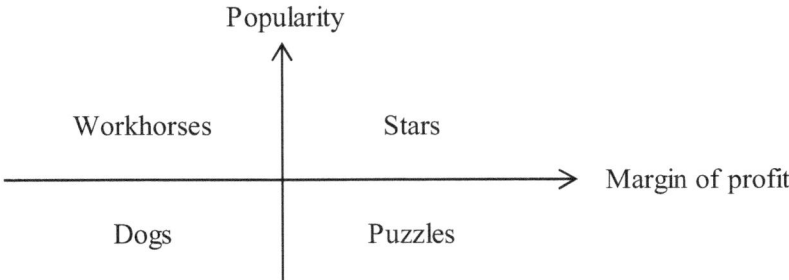

Figure 32: the visual representation of the classes.

Stars

- Stars are popular and have a high profit margin.
- *Be strict on MIS.*
- *Monitoring MIS. on regular basis.*
- *The best placement on menu*
- *Depending on price elasticity we should try to raise the price.*
- *Depending on originality in the market, raise price.*

- *Promote this item.*

- *Staff needs to recommend this item to customers.*

Workhorses

- Workhorses are popular but have a low profit margin.

- *Negotiate better prices for the ingredients.*

- *Can't be removed from the menu.*

- *Place on a different part of the menu (the least good place, to draw customers' attention to stars and puzzles).*

- *Revise MIS (portion sizes).*

- *Raise sales price slightly to increase profit (it's popular so people will keep ordering it).*

Puzzles

- Puzzles are not popular but have a high profit margin.

- *Promote this item (if done well it could become a star).*

- *Give this item a better placement on the menu.*

- *Staff needs to promote this item to customers.*

- *Change the name of the dish (make it more attractive).*

- *Lower the price on the menu (be careful).*

Dogs

Dogs are not popular and have a low profit margin.

- *This item has no business existing on the menu.*

- *Remove from menu if labor costs for this item are high, ingredients have a short shelf life or are not usable for waste processing, etc.*

- *Try to raise the sales price (make it a puzzle).*

Popular- and high profit items

To find out what item on the menu is popular we need to find the menu mix. This gives us the share of an item in terms of percentage on the total number of items sold. To find this percentage we use the following formula.

(Numbers of an item sold / total numbers of all items sold) x 100 = menu mix

This will give us a percentage per item (the sum of all percentages should of course be 100%).

To find the average menu mix we use the following formula.

100 / number of items on the menu = average menu mix

This does not tell us whether the dish is popular or not. To find out if the item is popular, we multiply the average menu mix with a certain percentage (free to choose). To rule out borderline items, 70% is a good percentage to go with. This will give you the popularity rate. The formula is the following one.

Average menu mix x chosen percentage (70%) = popularity rate

The items for which the menu mix is equal or higher than the popularity rate, are indeed popular.

To find out what item has a high profit margin we need to find the average profit margin first. To find the average profit margin we use the following formula.

Total profit margin / total number of items sold = average profit margin

All items that have a profit margin equal or higher than the average profit margin are indeed items that have a high profit margin.

In the figure below we find a complete analysis of a dessert menu. All the prices are net prices, except for the G.S.P. (gross sales price or price on the menu).

Desserts	G.S.P.	N.S.P.	Cof	Sold	MM	G. profit	Cof total	Rev. Tot.	G. profit Tot.	GP cat.	MM cat.	Class
Moelleux	€ 4,50	€ 3,60	€ 1,20	362	13,77%	€ 2,40	€ 434,40	€ 1.303,20	€ 868,80	low	high	Plow
Sorbet	€ 4,75	€ 3,80	€ 0,85	248	9,43%	€ 2,95	€ 210,80	€ 942,40	€ 731,60	low	high	Plow
Hazelnut cake	€ 4,75	€ 3,80	€ 1,10	145	5,52%	€ 2,70	€ 159,50	€ 551,00	€ 391,50	low	low	Dog
Chocolate mousse	€ 5,25	€ 4,20	€ 0,55	321	12,21%	€ 3,65	€ 176,55	€ 1.348,20	€ 1.171,65	high	high	Star
Crème caramel	€ 5,50	€ 4,40	€ 1,35	240	9,13%	€ 3,05	€ 324,00	€ 1.056,00	€ 732,00	low	high	Plow
Apple crisp	€ 5,50	€ 4,40	€ 1,40	358	13,62%	€ 3,00	€ 501,20	€ 1.575,20	€ 1.074,00	low	high	Plow
Sabayon	€ 6,50	€ 5,20	€ 0,70	243	9,24%	€ 4,50	€ 170,10	€ 1.263,60	€ 1.093,50	high	high	Star
Tiramisu	€ 7,00	€ 5,60	€ 1,25	120	4,56%	€ 4,35	€ 150,00	€ 672,00	€ 522,00	high	low	Puzzle
Red velvet cake	€ 7,50	€ 6,00	€ 1,50	402	15,29%	€ 4,50	€ 603,00	€ 2.412,00	€ 1.809,00	high	high	Star
Crème brulee	€ 8,00	€ 6,40	€ 1,05	190	7,23%	€ 5,35	€ 199,50	€ 1.216,00	€ 1.016,50	high	high	Star
Total	€ 59,25	€ 47,40	€ 10,95	2629	100%	€ 36,45	€ 2.929,05	€ 12.339,60	€ 9.410,55			
Average MM					10%							
Food cost							24%					
Average G. profit									€ 3,58			
70% on averag MM					7%							

Figure 33: the full overview of the dessert menu.

The figure above explained.

- *G.S.P. (gross sales price) = price on the menu.*

- *N.S.P. (net sales price) = gross sales price without the VAT (25% in this case).*

- *C.O.F. (cost of food) = cost of food based on MIS. (1 item).*

- *Sold = the actual times an item was sold.*

- *MM = menu mix. For moelleux this would be 13,77% (362 / 2.629 x 100).*

- *G. profit = net sales price – cost of food.*

- *C.O.F. total = cost of food x sold.*

- *Rev. total (revenue total) = net sales price x sold.*

- *G. profit tot. (gross profit total) = revenue total – cost of food total.*

- *Average MM (average menu mix) = 100 / number of items (100 / 10) = 10%.*

- *Food cost = cost of food total / revenue total.*

- *Average G. profit M. (average gross profit margin) = €9.410,55 / 2629 = €3,58*

- *70% on average MM (70% on average menu mix) = 10% x 70% = 7%*

In the figure above, all items that have a menu mix (MM) of at least 7% are popular and items with a profit margin of at least €3,58 have a high profit margin. This gives the 'high' and 'low' remarks per line. This allows us to determine what class an item is. Now we can take appropriate action.

It is impossible to have only stars on the menu.

Chapter 11
The variance analyses

With the variance analyses we can even better understand how our restaurant is operating. We are going to compare actual results with the budget or the standardization of sales prices, sales volume and more. The be able to perform these types of analyses it is important that standardization of expenses has been done and that we work with some form of forecasting.

We will discuss the following analyses.

- *The sales variance analysis.*

- *The cost variance analysis.*

- *The labor cost variance analysis.*

The sales variance analysis

The sales variance analysis will give us an understanding of how the revenue relates to the sales volume and the spending power of our customers. In other words, we want to know how much sales have impacted our revenue and how much the spending of guests has had an impact on the result. Based on the outcome we can decide to focus on sales, for instance launch a marketing campaign to in increase sales numbers. We could also focus on the how we could get customers to spend more money in our restaurant, for instance via the implementation of menu engineering.

For our restaurant we have the following dishes on the menu.

						Prime ICM
Meals	Sales price	Cof per Kg	Portion in g	Cost of food	Food cost
1 Steak	€ 18,00	€ 21,60	275	€ 5,94	33,00%
2 Salmon	€ 21,00	€ 25,20	230	€ 5,80	27,60%
3 Chicken	€ 14,00	€ 16,80	250	€ 4,20	30,00%
4 Vegan	€ 15,00	€ 18,00	300	€ 5,40	36,00%

Figure 34: the calculation of the food costs.

The cost of food for steak is €5,94 ((€21,60 / 1.000 g) x 275 g). The food cost for steak is 33% ((€5,94 / €18)) x 100).

The sales forecast for the month February (28 days) can be found below.

Meals	Forecast	February
1 Steak	28	784
2 Salmon	25	700
3 Chicken	21	588
4 Vegan	16	448
Total	90	2520

Figure 35: the sales forecast for February.

The overview of the menu item sheets, and the sales forecast of the menu so far looks like the figure below. Food cost has been calculated by using the prime-ingredient costing method (Prime ICM).

						Prime ICM	
Meals	Sales price	Cof per Kg	Portion in g	Cost of food	Food cost	February
1 Steak	€ 18,00	€ 21,60	275	€ 5,94	33,00%	784
2 Salmon	€ 21,00	€ 25,20	230	€ 5,80	27,60%	700
3 Chicken	€ 14,00	€ 16,80	250	€ 4,20	30,00%	588
4 Vegan	€ 15,00	€ 18,00	300	€ 5,40	36,00%	448

Figure 36: the overview of the MIS, and the sales forecast of the menu

In the next figure we can find the actual results for the month February. The actual results are always market in grey.

113

Meals	Sales price	Cof per Kg	Portion in g	Cost of food	Food cost	February
1 Steak	€ 17,50	€ 20,45	285	€ 5,83	33,30%	801
2 Salmon	€ 19,75	€ 26,35	235	€ 6,19	31,35%	688
3 Chicken	€ 13,00	€ 16,40	265	€ 4,35	33,43%	594
4 Vegan	€ 14,25	€ 17,80	315	€ 5,61	39,35%	445

Figure 37: the actual results for the month February.

Now let us have a look at the revenue forecast and the actual revenue for this month. We can find the results in the figure below.

Meals	Sales price	February	Revenue
1 Steak	€ 18,00	784	€ 14.112,00
2 Salmon	€ 21,00	700	€ 14.700,00
3 Chicken	€ 14,00	588	€ 8.232,00
4 Vegan	€ 15,00	448	€ 6.720,00
	Total	2520	€ 43.764,00

Meals	Sales price	February	Revenue
1 Steak	€ 17,50	801	€ 14.017,50
2 Salmon	€ 19,75	688	€ 13.588,00
3 Chicken	€ 13,00	594	€ 7.722,00
4 Vegan	€ 14,25	445	€ 6.341,25
	Total	2528	€ 41.668,75
	Difference		€ -2.095,25

Figure 38: the revenue forecast compared to the actual revenue.

A few things are noticeable. The sales prices that were set on the menu (without VAT) are different from the prices that have been paid for these meals. This is due to discounts because this will reduce the average sales price of an item. Normally the average sales price per item should be the exact same price as shown on the menu.

For steak @ €18 we should generate €18 per sale, in this case we were expecting to earn €14.112 (€18 x 784).

According to the actual results we have only earned €17,50 per steak sold, that is €0,50 less per steak (€18 – €17,50).

Not only are the sales prices different. We can also see that the expected sales numbers (volume) are different from the actual sales numbers.

For steak we were expecting to sell 784 meals, we have sold 801 meals. We have sold an additional 17 steak meals (801 – 784).

The actual revenue for steak is €14.017,50 (€17,50 x 801).

For the steak meal we see that we have sold more than forecasted, but we have sold at a cheaper price.

If we look at the total numbers from the budget and the actual numbers, we notice that we have sold 2.528 meals, 8 more than expected (2.528 – 2.520) and generated €41.668,75 instead of the expected €43.764, that is €2.095,25 (€43.764 – €41.668,75) less.

Even though we did sell 8 extra meals, we still received €2.095,25 less in revenue. The reason for this is because of a difference in sales prices and sales numbers.

The sales volume

To understand how impactful the difference in sales volume is, we can use the following formula.

(Budget sales – actual sales) x standard sales price per item = sales volume

Meals	Sales price	February	February	Difference	Revenue
1 Steak	€ 18,00	784	801	-17	€ -306,00
2 Salmon	€ 21,00	700	688	12	€ 252,00
3 Chicken	€ 14,00	588	594	-6	€ -84,00
4 Vegan	€ 15,00	448	445	3	€ 45,00
			Total	-8	€ -93,00

Figure 39: the impact of sales volume on the revenue.

In the figure above we see the impact of the sales volume per item.

For steak, the impact of more sales has increased revenue for steak by €306 ((784 – 801) x €18).

The total number of sales, in this case an additional 8 meals has had a positive impact on the revenue. We have earned an additional €93 because of these 8 extra meals sold. This is positive for the restaurant.

The spending power

To understand how much impact the differences in sales prices have on the actual revenue we can use the following formula.

(Sales price per item – actual sales price per item) x actual sales = spending power

Meals	Sales price	Sales price	February	Difference	Revenue
1 Steak	€ 18,00	€ 17,50	801	€ 0,50	€ 400,50
2 Salmon	€ 21,00	€ 19,75	688	€ 1,25	€ 860,00
3 Chicken	€ 14,00	€ 13,00	594	€ 1,00	€ 594,00
4 Vegan	€ 15,00	€ 14,25	445	€ 0,75	€ 333,75
			Total	€ 3,50	€ 2.188,25

Figure 40: the impact of the purchasing price differences.

For steak, the difference of €0,50 less, has made a negative impact on the revenue of €400,50 ((€18 - €17,50) x 801).

For all items combined this means that the difference in sales prices have had a negative impact on the revenue of €2.188,25. This is negative for the restaurant.

In this example the negative variance of €2.095,25 is caused by us selling items at lower prices. We must take a closer look at why we are selling at lower prices. Are guests not happy with the quality? Discounts due to advertising? Are we working with price fences?

Meals	Budget revenue	Volume	Spending power	Actual revenue
1 Steak	€ 14.112,00	€ -306,00	€ 400,50	€ 14.017,50
2 Salmon	€ 14.700,00	€ 252,00	€ 860,00	€ 13.588,00
3 Chicken	€ 8.232,00	€ -84,00	€ 594,00	€ 7.722,00
4 Vegan	€ 6.720,00	€ 45,00	€ 333,75	€ 6.341,25
	€ 43.764,00	€ -93,00	€ 2.188,25	€ 41.668,75
	+	-	-	=
	Plus	Plus	Minus	Plus

Figure 41: the overview of the sales variance analysis.

In the figure above we can see the result for the sales variance analysis.

The cost variance analysis

Now that we understand what is going on with the sales of our restaurant, we can have a look at the costs. With the cost variance analysis, we can figure out how well we are managing the direct costs of the production. We are talking about food costs and beverage costs.

Meals	Sales price	Cof per Kg	Portion in g	Cost of food	Food cost	February	Total cost of food
1 Steak	€ 18,00	€ 21,60	275	€ 5,94	33,00%	784	€ 4.656,96
2 Salmon	€ 21,00	€ 25,20	230	€ 5,80	27,60%	700	€ 4.057,20
3 Chicken	€ 14,00	€ 16,80	250	€ 4,20	30,00%	588	€ 2.469,60
4 Vegan	€ 15,00	€ 18,00	300	€ 5,40	36,00%	448	€ 2.419,20
				Total	126,60%	2520	€ 13.602,96
				Average	31,65%		

Meals	Sales price	Cof per Kg	Portion in g	Cost of food	Food cost	February	Total cost of food
1 Steak	€ 17,50	€ 20,45	285	€ 5,83	33,30%	801	€ 4.668,43
2 Salmon	€ 19,75	€ 26,35	235	€ 6,19	31,35%	688	€ 4.260,27
3 Chicken	€ 13,00	€ 16,40	265	€ 4,35	33,43%	594	€ 2.581,52
4 Vegan	€ 14,25	€ 17,80	315	€ 5,61	39,35%	445	€ 2.495,12
				Total	137,44%	2528	€ 14.005,34
				Average	34,36%		
						Difference	€ -402,38

Figure 42: the food cost comparison between the budget- and actual results.

In the figure above we can see the budget and the actual results for the generated costs based on the sales numbers.

To produce 1 steak meal, we need to spend €5,94 (33% food cost). If we expect to sell 784 steak meals the total cost of food for steak should be €4.656,96 (€5,94 x 784). The total expected cost of food for February is €13.602,96 (the sum of all items). The average food cost for the whole menu is expected to be 31,65% ((33% + 27,60% + 30% + 36%) / 4). However, it is better to use the total cost of food and the total revenue, this would give us a target food cost of 31,08% ((€13.602,96 / €43.764) x 100).

We can already see that we've spend €402,38 more on the production of meals. There are 2 reasons why this could have happened. We could have used more (portion sizes), or the purchasing prices have changed with our suppliers, or a combination of both. We can see that for some meals we have had better purchasing prices and we can see that for all meals we did not respect the menu item sheets, we have served larger portions (portion in gram).

The cost volume

By calculating a cost volume, we can figure out how the sales volume (sold meals) have impacted the costs of production (food cost and beverage cost). We try find an answer to the question whether the surplus, or deficit in costs (the difference between expected- and actual sales) was the main contributor to the overall increase or decrease in production costs.

To find out how much this difference had an impact we can use the following formula.

(Expected sales – actual sales) x expected cost of food per item

Meals	February	February	Cost of food		Difference		Total cost of food
1 Steak	784	801	€	5,94	-17	€	-100,98
2 Salmon	700	688	€	5,80	12	€	69,55
3 Chicken	588	594	€	4,20	-6	€	-25,20
4 Vegan	448	445	€	5,40	3	€	16,20
	2520	2528			-8	€	-40,43

Figure 43: the cost of the sales volume.

For steak we find a negative result of €100,98 ((784 – 801) x €5,94). This means that the 17 additional steak meals we have sold, generated an additional €100,98 (€5,94 x 17) cost of food. This is negative because it increases the total cost of food.

In the case of the salmon meal, we can see that the 12 meals we have sold less, is saving us €69,55 (€5,80 x 12) because we do not have to prepare these meals, therefor we do not have to spend €5,80 per produced meal.

In total the 8 additional meals we have sold in February are costing us an additional €40,43. This is not necessarily a problem because we need to make costs to generate revenue. If we sell more, we need to produce more and spend more money on ingredients, however we should also (hopefully) generate more revenue to justify additional costs.

The cost of food- and beverage price

In this part we are going to find out how much the purchasing prices, or more specifically how the differences in purchasing prices play a role in the overall increase or decrease in costs. If we have paid less this will have positive effect on the costs (decrease) and if we have paid more, it would have a negative impact on the costs (increase).

We can use the following formula to find the answers.

(Expected cost of food – actual cost of food) x actual sales = cost of food price

Meals	Cof per Kg		Cof per Kg	February Portion in g	Cof difference	Portion in Kg	Kg used	Total cof difference
1 Steak	€ 21,60	€	20,45	801	285 €	1,15	0,285	228,29 €	262,53
2 Salmon	€ 25,20	€	26,35	688	235 €	-1,15	0,235	161,68 €	-185,93
3 Chicken	€ 16,80	€	16,40	594	265 €	0,40	0,265	157,41 €	62,96
4 Vegan	€ 18,00	€	17,80	445	315 €	0,20	0,315	140,18 €	28,03
							Total €		167,59

Figure 44: the cost of food impact because of purchase price differences.

For steak we paid €1,15 less per kg (€21,60 – €20,45), this is positive for the restaurant because purchasing steak is cheaper than expected. However, we have used larger portion sizes, this means that some of this benefit will be lost because of it.

We have purchased 228,29 kg steak (0,285 kg x 801) to produce 801 meals. This means that we have saved €262,53 (€1,15 x 228,29 kg) on purchasing steak. For every kilogram we have bought we save €1,15. In total we saved €167,59 because of lower purchasing prices. As we can see only the salmon was more expensive. If we could get a better price for salmon, we could save even more on purchasing.

We can safely say that we are doing an excellent job in keeping purchase prices under control and that the cheaper prices are contributing to better profit margins.

The cost of food and beverage usage

In this part we can figure out how much impact the difference between the expected usage (portion sizes) and the actual usage is. We know that we have made more ingredient costs than expected. We also know that the additional sold meals contributed to this total cost of food being higher and the cheaper purchasing prices contributed to this cost being lower. Let us have look if our portion

120

sizes have had a positive or negative impact on the total cost of food.

We can use the formula below.

((Expected cost of food per item x actual sales) – (actual sales cost of food x actual cost of food per item)) x expected cost of food = usage

Meals	Cof per Kg	Cof per Kg February	Portion in Kg	Portion in Kg	Budget @ actual Kg	Actual @ actual Kg	Difference in Kg	Difference
1 Steak	€ 21,60	€ 20,45	801	0,275	0,285	220,28	228,29	-8,01 € -173,02
2 Salmon	€ 25,20	€ 26,35	688	0,230	0,235	158,24	161,68	-3,44 € -86,69
3 Chicken	€ 16,80	€ 16,40	594	0,250	0,265	148,50	157,41	-8,91 € -149,69
4 Vegan	€ 18,00	€ 17,80	445	0,300	0,315	133,50	140,18	-6,68 € -120,15
						Total		€ -529,54

Figure 45: the impact of usage on the cost of food.

For our steak meal we are expected to use 275 g or 0,275 kg. If we served each guest exactly this portion size, we should have used 220,28 kg of steak (0,275 kg x 801). We have served each guest 285 g per meal. This means for each meal sold we serve an additional 10 g, or in other words we need to buy an additional 10 g from our supplier. The actual purchased weight is 228,29 kg (0,285 kg x 801). This is a difference of 8,01 kg (228,29 kg – 220,28 kg).

The fact that we have served slightly larger portions is costing us and additional €173,02 (€20,45 x 8,01 kg).

In total we've spend an additional €529,54 since we do not respect the menu item sheets (or the recipe). This is the main reason our food cost is much higher that forecasted. We need to address this problem with the kitchen staff. Why are they serving larger portions? If we can solve this issue, we can reduce the food cost significantly.

Meals	Total cost of food		Cost volume		Cost of food price		Cost of food usage		Total cost of food
1 Steak	€	4.656,96	€	-100,98	€	262,53	€	-173,02	€	4.668,43
2 Salmon	€	4.057,20	€	69,55	€	-185,93	€	-86,69	€	4.260,27
3 Chicken	€	2.469,60	€	-25,20	€	62,96	€	-149,69	€	2.581,52
4 Vegan	€	2.419,20	€	16,20	€	28,03	€	-120,15	€	2.495,12
	€	13.602,96	€	-40,43	€	167,59	€	-529,54	€	14.005,34
	+		-		-		-		=
	Plus		Plus		Minus		Plus		Plus

Figure 46: the overview of the cost variance analysis.

As we can see in the overview of the cost variance analysis, additional sales increased the costs by €40,43 and the lower purchasing prices decreased the cost of food by €167,59 and the lack of portion control increased the cost of food by €529,54.

The result is an actual cost of food of €14.005,34 (€13.602,96 + €40,43 – €167,59 + €529,54).

The labor cost variance analysis

The last direct costs we can have a look at are the direct labor costs. We want to find out how an increase, or decrease in sales impacts the costs of labor, how well we have managed the expected hourly wages and how efficient our kitchen team is working. We will have look at, volume, costs, and efficiency.

While we do need to have look at the labor costs, we do need to keep in mind that we are comparing wages directly to the number of items produced. This is not 100% fair since kitchen staff is not always producing meals. Things like coaching, cleaning, ordering, designing menus and more should be considered. However, based on the results of this analysis we can ask the right questions. Why are they coaching so much? Why do they spend so much time on ordering ingredients?

We assume that we know how much each kitchen employee earns (fixed salary or hourly wage). We know how many hours each staff member is supposed to work according to the forecast, and we are aware that overtime, weekend work and so on cost more in wages.

Number	Title	Salary	Hours per week	February hours	Salary per hour
1	Chef	€ 5.000,00	40	160	€ 31,25
1	Cook	€ 2.500,00	40	160	€ 15,63
1	Cook	€ 1.000,00	16	64	€ 15,63
1	Cook	€ 1.000,00	16	64	€ 15,63
1	Cleaner	€ 1.600,00	40	160	€ 10,00
1	Cleaner	€ 640,00	16	64	€ 10,00
6		€ 11.740,00	168	672	€ 17,47

Number	Title	Salary	Hours per week	February hours	Salary per hour
1	Chef	€ 5.900,00	45	180	€ 32,78
1	Cook	€ 2.800,00	45	180	€ 15,56
1	Cook	€ 1.450,00	21	84	€ 17,26
1	Cook	€ 1.450,00	21	84	€ 17,26
1	Cleaner	€ 1.950,00	45	180	€ 10,83
1	Cleaner	€ 925,00	21	84	€ 11,01
6		€ 14.475,00	198	792	€ 18,28

Figure 47: the salary overview of the kitchen staff.

In the figure above we can find the expected labor costs according to what each employee is getting paid, and we can find the actual results as well.

We expected the chef to work 40 hours per week or 160 hours during February. The chef has a salary of €31,25 per hour (€5.000 / 160). The chef worked 180 hours and we paid €5.900 (overtime, etc. included). This brings the actual hourly wage up to €32,78 (€5.900 / 180).

In total we were expecting to pay €11.740 in wages and have a budgeted salary per hour of €17,47 (€11.740 / 672).

The actual results for February are different from the budget. We have spent €2.735 (€11.740 – €14.475) more on wages and the hourly salary rate is €0,81 (€17,47 – €18,28) more.

In the figure below we can see the expected production times and the actual production times of each meal on the menu.

Meals	February	Standard salary rate	Production time	Minutes Total production time	Hours Total production time	Standard labor cost
1 Steak	784 €	17,47	7	5488	91,47 €	1.597,94
2 Salmon	700 €	17,47	9	6300	105,00 €	1.834,38
3 Chicken	588 €	17,47	6	3528	58,80 €	1.027,25
4 Vegan	448 €	17,47	9	4032	67,20 €	1.174,00
	2520 €	17,47		19348	322,47 €	5.633,57

Meals	February	Actual salary rate	Production time	Total production time	Total production time	Actual labor cost
1 Steak	801 €	18,28	9	7209	120,15 €	2.195,92
2 Salmon	688 €	18,28	11	7568	126,13 €	2.305,28
3 Chicken	594 €	18,28	9	5346	89,10 €	1.628,44
4 Vegan	445 €	18,28	8	3560	59,33 €	1.084,41
	2528 €	18,28		23683	394,72 €	7.214,05

Figure 48: the overview of the forecasted production times.

For the steak meal we have estimated, according to the menu item sheet, that it takes 7 minutes to produce this item. We were expecting to sell 784 meals which would bring the total production time to 5.488 minutes (7' x 784) or 91,47 hours (5.488' / 60).

If the standard or the expected salary cost per hour is €17,47, then the total expected labor cost is €1.597,94 (€17,47 x 91,47). We were expecting to pay €5.633,57 to produce all meals, however we have spent €1.580,48 (€7.214,05 – €5.633,57) more. This is caused by the fact that we've spend an additional 72,25 (394,72 – 322,47) hours on the production. As we can see the production time for each meal is different than we have expected.

The volume

The result of this analysis tells us whether we have spent more on labor costs or less due to more, or less produced meals.

The formula we can use is the following.

(Expected sales – actual sales) x (total standard labor cost per item / expected sales) = volume

Meals	February	February	Difference meals	Standard labor cost		Standard cost per meal		Difference
1 Steak	784	801	-17 €	1.597,94	€	2,04	€	-34,65
2 Salmon	700	688	12 €	1.834,38	€	2,62	€	31,45
3 Chicken	588	594	-6 €	1.027,25	€	1,75	€	-10,48
4 Vegan	448	445	3 €	1.174,00	€	2,62	€	7,86
	2520	2528	-8 €	5.633,57	€	9,03	€	-5,82

Figure 49: the impact of sales on the labor cost.

For the steak we find a difference of €34,65 ((784 – 801) x (€1.597,94 / 784)) or (17 x €2,04). This is negative for the restaurant. We spend €34,65 more on the production of steaks since we sell 17 more meals.

In total we've spend €5,82 (-€34,65 + €31,45 – €10,48 + €7,86) more on labor costs because of the distribution of meals sold and the eventual difference of 8 extra meals sold.

The cost price per hour

In this part we can figure out what the impact of the actual hourly salary is on the total production. In other words, how much did we need to pay more, or less due to higher, or lower wages caused by an increase, or decrease in production time. The main factor is the actual increase or decrease in salary.

The formula we can us to calculate this is the following one.

(Standard salary per hour – actual salary per hour) x actual hours worked = cost price per hour

Meals	Standard salary rate		Actual salary rate		Total production time		Rate difference	Price cost	
1 Steak	€	17,47	€	18,28	120,15	€	-0,81	€	-96,87
2 Salmon	€	17,47	€	18,28	126,13	€	-0,81	€	-101,70
3 Chicken	€	17,47	€	18,28	89,10	€	-0,81	€	-71,84
4 Vegan	€	17,47	€	18,28	59,33	€	-0,81	€	-47,84
	€	17,47	€	18,28	394,72	€	-0,81	€	-318,25

Figure 50: the impact of the salary rate difference.

We know that the difference between budget salary and actual salary per hour is €0,81. We also know what the actual production time per item has been.

For steak there was an increase in labor cost of €96,87 ((€17,47 – €18,28) x 120,15) since we are paying an additional €0,81 salary per worked hour.

In total we've spend €318,25 more on salary because of this increase in salary of €0,81. This however is only 20,14% ((€318,25 / €1.580,48) x 100) of the €1.580,48 more spend on salaries. As we might expect the problem is going to be efficiency.

The efficiency

With the efficiency calculation we can determine whether our kitchen staff is working efficient or not. In other words, are they meeting the expected production times or are they working faster or slower than expected.

To find the answers we can use the following formula.

((Expected production time x actual sales) – actual production time) x standard hourly rate = efficiency cost

Meals	February	Production time	Total production time	Total production time	Standard salary rate	Difference	Efficiency cost
1 Steak	801	7	120,15	93,45 €	17,47	-26,70 €	-466,46
2 Salmon	688	9	126,13	103,20 €	17,47	-22,93 €	-400,65
3 Chicken	594	6	89,10	59,40 €	17,47	-29,70 €	-518,87
4 Vegan	445	9	59,33	66,75 €	17,47	7,42 €	129,57
	2528		394,72	322,80 €	17,47	-71,92 €	-1.256,40

Figure 51: the cost of efficiency.

For steak we find an efficiency cost of €466,46 (((7' x 801) – 120,15) x €17,47) or ((93,45 – 120,15) x €17,47). This means that because we have spent 26,70 (120,15 – 93,45) hours longer on the production of steaks we must pay €466,46 more in wages, this is negative. In other words, production is slower than expected. This

126

is what that extra 2 minutes of preparation time is costing us (7' – 9'). Only for the vegan meals the kitchen staff works more efficiently.

In total the kitchen staff is not as efficient as was expected. We have spent an additional €1.256,40 (-€466,40 – €400,65 – 518,87 + €129,57) because of inefficiency.

We need to find out why production was much slower of course. This might have several reasons. They we were understaffed, unforeseen circumstances or the budgeted production time was too strict. While we see less efficiency in our kitchen based on the numbers, this does not mean that employees are not working as hard as they can.

Meals	Standard labor cost	Volume	Cost price	Efficiency	Actual labor cost
1 Steak	€ 1.597,94	€ -34,65	€ -96,87	€ -466,46	€ 2.195,92
2 Salmon	€ 1.834,38	€ 31,45	€ -101,70	€ -400,65	€ 2.305,28
3 Chicken	€ 1.027,25	€ -10,48	€ -71,84	€ -518,87	€ 1.628,44
4 Vegan	€ 1.174,00	€ 7,86	€ -47,84	€ 129,57	€ 1.084,41
	€ 5.633,57	€ -5,82	€ -318,25	€ -1.256,40	€ 7.214,05
	+	-	-	-	
	Plus	Plus	Plus	Plus	

Figure 52: the overview of the labor cost variance analysis.

As we can see in the overview of the labor cost variance analysis, we have lost money due to volume, paying more salary per hour and being less efficient. The result is an actual labor cost of €7.214,05 (€5.633,57 + €5,82 + €318,25 + 1.256,40). The difference of €1.580,48 is caused by inefficiency.

The result of the variance analyses

Now that we have calculated all the variances, we can take action to increase the actual results for the next period. As we now understand it is important to keep track of these variances to understand more specifically where potential problems can arise. In the figure below we can see the result for the restaurant in terms of net profit if there was a profit tax of 25%.

The fact that we have underperformed on sales and direct expenses has led to a negative difference of €3.924,47 in profit.

	Forecast	Actual
Sales	€ 43.764,00	€ 41.668,75
Cost of food	€ 13.602,96	€ 14.005,34
Salaries	€ 11.740,00	€ 14.475,00
Other	€ -	€ -
Gross profit	€ 18.421,04	€ 13.188,41
Taxes	€ 4.605,26	€ 3.297,10
Net profit	€ 13.815,78	€ 9.891,31
Difference	€ -3.924,47	

Figure 53: the revenue overview of the restaurant.